CONTENTS

▲ *Solomon in the Temple Treasury* by Frans Franken II (1633)

▲ *The Sacrifice of Isaac* by Laurent de La Hyre (17th century)

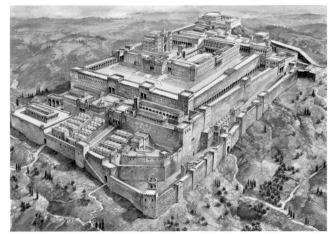

▲ *Solomon's Palace and Temple in Jerusalem* by an unknown artist (ca. 1900)

NEW TESTAMENT

▲ *The Holy Family*
by Anton Raphael Mengs (1749)

▲ *Crucifixion with God the Father and Saint Ignatius of Loyola*
by Francesco Fontebasso (ca. 18th century)

▲ *St. Paul and St. Barnabas in Listri*
by Simone Peterzano (16th century)

INTRODUCTION

Beautiful paintings and illustrations, many from well-known artists

One of the most influential and inspiring books ever written, the Bible has been studied for more than two millennia for its historical and theological significance, for its commandments and laws, and for its poetry and prose.

At the heart of both the Old and New Testaments are moving and timeless human stories. There are tales of kings, judges, and prophets; of teachers and disciples; of the strong and the meek, the wicked and the innocent. They are people whose ancient experiences provide everyday wisdom for living in the modern era.

Adam and Eve, yielding to temptation in the Garden of Eden, learn they must pay the consequences for exercising free will. David is a fearless warrior, but as king he becomes reckless in his personal life and is cursed with a rebellious son. While dying on the cross and suffering profoundly, Jesus asks God to forgive his persecutors.

Everything You Need to Know About the Bible brings together these essential stories in a beautiful, easy-to-read guide that sheds fresh light on the Bible for readers of all spiritual backgrounds. There are unique features such as the **Verse to Know**, which identifies famous, inspirational passages. **Timelines** put the Bible's narrative in historical context, while **maps** provide a geographical reference. There are gorgeously reproduced works of art to help the reader consider even the most familiar tales in a new way and **What's in a Name** boxes to explain the etymology behind many well-known biblical characters.

With interfaith perspectives, *Everything You Need to Know About the Bible* touches each book in the Old and New Testaments, highlighting key chapters and concepts. Here truly are the essential people, stories, dates, messages, and scripture references from the New Revised Standard Version. This book does not attempt to untangle thousands of years of debate and controversy about the Bible. Instead, it provides insight into biblical scholarship and theology to help you decide for yourself.

Whether you are already familiar with the Bible's contents or completely new to its teachings, *Everything You Need to Know About the Bible* will help you navigate and understand this magnificent book's eternal lessons.

Fact-filled captions

Bible chapter citations for easy cross-referencing

Maps that provide geographical context

Informative timelines

Focus on special events and dates

Helpful sidebars and scholarly perspective

Verse to Know highlighting key passages

CHAPTER 1

IN THE BEGINNING . . .

Genesis is the first book in the Hebrew Bible, or the Old Testament. It opens with the well-known phrase, "In the beginning . . ." which is appropriate because the word *genesis* means "origin" or "beginning."

The book introduces the deity called God or the Lord, his creation, and his relationship with the first humans.

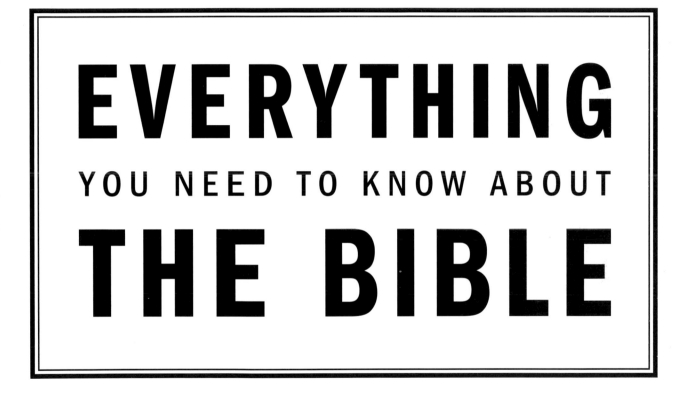

EVERYTHING

YOU NEED TO KNOW ABOUT

THE BIBLE

Editors Eileen Daspin, Michael Solomon
Consulting Designer Ryan Moore

Time Home Entertainment

Publisher Jim Childs
Vice President, Brand & Digital Strategy Steven Sandonato
Executive Director, Marketing Services Carol Pittard
Executive Director, Retail & Special Sales Tom Mifsud
Executive Publishing Director Joy Bomba
Director, Bookazine Development & Marketing Laura Adam
Vice President, Finance Vandana Patel
Publishing Director Megan Pearlman
Assistant General Counsel Simone Procas
Assistant Director, Special Sales Ilene Schreider
Senior Book Production Manager Susan Chodakiewicz
Brand Manager Katie McHugh Malm
Associate Prepress Manager Alex Voznesenskiy
Associate Project Manager Stephanie Braga

Editorial Director Stephen Koepp
Senior Editor Roe D'Angelo
Copy Chief Rina Bander
Design Manager Anne-Michelle Gallero
Editorial Operations Gina Scauzillo

SPECIAL THANKS
Katherine Barnet, Brad Beatson, Jeremy Biloon, Rose Cirrincione, Natalie
Ebel, Assu Etsubneh, Mariana Evans, Christine Font, Susan Hettleman,
Hillary Hirsch, David Kahn, Mona Li, Amy Mangus, Kimberly Marshall,
Nina Mistry, Dave Rozzelle, Ricardo Santiago, Adriana Tierno

Copyright © 2014 Time Home Entertainment Inc.

Published by Time Home Entertainment Inc.
135 West 50th Street • New York, NY 10020

New Revised Standard Version Bible, copyright 1989, Division of Christian
Education of the National Council of the Churches of Christ in the United
States of America. Used by permission. All rights reserved.

ISBN 10: 1-60320-996-4
ISBN 13: 978-1-60320-996-0

We welcome your comments and suggestions about Time Home
Entertainment Books. Please write to us at:
Time Home Entertainment Books, Attention: Book Editors,
P.O. Box 11016, Des Moines, IA 50336-1016.
If you would like to order any of our hardcover Collector's Edition books,
please call us at 1-800-327-6388, Monday through Friday,
7 a.m.–8 p.m., or Saturday, 7 a.m.–6 p.m., Central Time.

Produced by **Contentra Technologies**

Project Manager Jon Bogart
Writers Cheryl Frey, Sandie Griffin,
Rick Presley, Elizabeth Smith
Designer Ritu Chopra
Photo Researcher Nivisha Sinha
Special Thanks Himanshu Chawla, Md. Furqan, Ella Hanna,
Rakesh Kumar, Indrajeet Kumar, Prabhat Rastogi, Leslie Jenkins Reed,
Lisa Slone, and Sudhakar Rout

Last Judgment by Jean Cousin the Younger (1585)

GENESIS 1

The Big Question: Where Do We Come From?

THE FIRST CHAPTERS ADDRESS IMPORTANT
ISSUES ABOUT THE HUMAN CONDITION.

Genesis lays the foundation for tackling the big questions in life. It uses the medium of narrative story—setting, characters, and plot—to present answers to the deeper philosophical questions of origin.

The story appears rather simple, but in the space of four chapters, it introduces us to some big ideas:

- the beginning of the universe
- the origin of life
- the question of evil
- the reason for death and suffering
- the interplay of humans and nature
- the connection of humans to fellow humans
- the relationship of humans to God

One of the great achievements of the Bible is that it deals with these and other grand themes with such a small amount of narrative text. One can read the first five chapters of Genesis in a few minutes and spend a lifetime pondering its implications.

Three of the world's major religions–Judaism, Christianity, and Islam–all look to Genesis to explain the origins of their faith and their existence.

Illustrated panels from a 15th-century copy of Boccaccio's *De Casibus Virorum Illustrium*, which recounted stories from the Bible.

WHO WROTE THE TORAH?

Traditionally Jewish and Christian scholars have taught that Moses wrote the Torah, the first five books of the Bible, except for the verses at the end of Deuteronomy.

This leads to the question of how Moses knew what to say about Creation since he could not have been present during those events. Judaism holds that God dictated to Moses.

More recent scholarship favors the theory that Moses or a later editor compiled the accounts in Genesis into a single book known as the Torah.

What is unquestionable is that the stories themselves are ancient in their origin and have been a rich part of Hebrew life for millenia.

The Days of Creation

Day 1
Genesis 1:3-5 **LIGHT** God establishes day and night.

Day 2
Genesis 1:6-8 **SKY** God sets a dome to separate the earth below from the heavens above.

Day 3
Genesis 1:9-13 **EARTH** God divides dry land from the sea and fills the earth with vegetation.

Day 4
Genesis 1:14-19 **SUN, MOON, AND STARS** God creates bearers of the light to rule over the day and night.

Day 5
Genesis 1:20-23 **BIRDS AND SEA WILDLIFE** God fills the sea and sky with wildlife.

Day 6
Genesis 1:24-31 **ANIMAL LIFE AND MAN** God creates terrestrial creatures.

Day 7
Genesis 2:1-3 **SABBATH** God rests.

▲ *God Creating the World by Compass* from a 15th-century illustrated manuscript.

CREATION (GENESIS 1, 2)

Most ancient creation stories begin with the existence of matter, usually in a chaotic state, and then a variety of gods and goddesses initiate creation. Genesis states, *"In the beginning when God created the heavens and the earth, the earth was a formless void and darkness covered the face of the deep, while a wind from God swept over the face of the waters." (Genesis 1:1, 2)* In Genesis, a monotheistic God exists prior to any creative activity, which is a decided contrast to Egyptian and Canaanite creation stories.

The Creation of Adam is one of the center panels from Michelangelo's fresco on the ceiling of the Sistine Chapel—at that time, the Pope's private sanctuary in the Vatican. (ca. 1510)

THE WORLD WAS . . . ROUND?

Modern readers of the Bible are sometimes confused by the writing because information taken for granted today was unknown at the time. Likewise, readers from ancient times possessed knowledge they considered too obvious to require explanation. Genesis 1:6-8 is one such example. The early understanding of the cosmos was that the sphere was composed of a solid dome that contained the sun, moon, stars, and other bodies. Beneath the dome, the earth was a flat disk that floated on a vast sea. The account of creation in the Hebrew Bible makes sense once considered from the perspective of its intended audience.

▲ In Dutch master Hieronymus Bosch's *The Garden of Earthly Delights* creation is depicted behind a set of closed doors. (1603)

SEEING DOUBLE IN GENESIS

Throughout Genesis 1 and 2, ideas are paired and repeated to underscore their relationship to creation.

The Cosmos: On Day 1 God separates light from dark. On Day 4 he populates light and dark with light bearers.

The Firmament: On Day 2 God separates the waters beneath the earth from the waters above the earth. On Day 5 he populates the sea and sky.

The Earth: On Day 3 God separates the land from the sea. On Day 6 he populates it with animals and man.

Jan Brueghel the Elder cleverly foreshadows the fall of Adam and Eve in the background of *The Temptation in the Garden of Eden.* (ca. 1600)

GENESIS 2:5-14

The Garden of Eden

GOD CREATES AN EARTHLY PARADISE.

This account opens with a description of a bare earth. There is no vegetation, no rain, and no one to till the ground. God then creates a human body out of the dust and breathes life into it.

This simple passage is of theological significance, since the body will return to earth some day, but the spirit will belong to God forever.

God then plants an earthly paradise called Eden and gives life to the first humans, Adam and Eve, to till and keep it. However, God also sows the seeds of humanity's ruin in the same garden by planting a tree of knowledge of good and evil and forbidding Adam to eat from it.

Theologians and scholars have speculated for centuries as to why God does this, and the matter remains unsettled for some. The general consensus is that God provides humans with a choice between good and evil, thus giving them a free will.

It is interesting to note that even though Western artists have typically portrayed the fruit as an apple, there is nothing in the text that suggests this.

It is quite possibly a play on the Latin word *malum*, which means both "evil" and "apple." From the beginning of the early church until the Protestant Reformation, most copies of the Bible were written in Latin, and artists may have been using a visual pun by portraying fruit of the tree of knowledge of good and evil (malum) as an apple (malum).

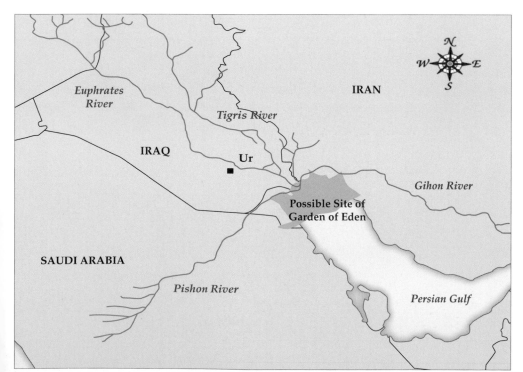

WHERE WAS THE GARDEN OF EDEN?

The description in Genesis 2:10-14 situates the Garden of Eden in "the East" at the headwaters of four great rivers—the Pishon, the Gihon, the Tigris, and the Euphrates.

While the Tigris and Euphrates rivers still flow in the Middle East, there is no consensus on the location of the Pishon and Gihon rivers. As a result, it is hard to pin down exactly where Eden was located. Some scholars speculate it was near the head of the Persian Gulf in modern-day Iraq, where the Tigris and Euphrates rivers meet.

Since the events of the first 12 chapters of Genesis take place in the Fertile Crescent, it naturally would follow that Eden would be located near Babylon and Ur, both of which are in Mesopotamia.

GENESIS 2:15–3:35

Adam and Eve:
From Innocence to Exile

THE FIRST HUMANS LEARN THAT KNOWLEDGE COMES AT A PRICE.

———————

All is not paradise in the Garden of Eden. God notices that man is alone and states that this is not good. According to the story, God brings creatures to Adam so that Adam can name them—which he does.

When Adam finishes naming all the animals, God notes that none are identified as man's helper. So he sends Adam to sleep, removes a rib, and creates a woman from it. He then presents her to Adam, who promptly identifies her as woman, "for out of man this one was taken." The woman is not called Eve until the next chapter.

Here, the text indicates the basis for marriage. Husband and wife are described as becoming "one flesh," an allusion both to the creative act and Adam's declaration about Eve.

The innocence of the first man and woman is emphasized by the statement that they were both naked and not embarrassed by it. This has practical and theological significance in the next chapter.

"So God created humankind in his image, in the image of God he created them . . ." (Gen. 1:27)

THE FALL FROM GRACE (GENESIS 3:1-24)

What was life like in the Garden of Eden before the Fall and how long did it last? Curiously, the Hebrew Bible is silent on this topic. Much of what is believed about life in Eden is presumed from what Adam and Eve lost in the Fall.

The narrative goes directly from the creation of the first couple to the commission of original sin.

The stage had been set for a conflict by God's command in Genesis 2:16, 17:

VERSE TO KNOW

"I heard the sound of you in the garden, and I was afraid, because I was naked; and I hid myself." (Gen. 3:10)

"You may freely eat of every tree of the garden; but of the tree of the knowledge of good and evil you shall not eat, for in the day that you eat of it you shall die." Chapter 3 opens with a new character, the serpent.

The Hebrew Bible offers no description other than to say the snake was craftier than any other wild animal. The serpent begins conversing with the woman, who does not appear to find the talking animal remarkable or even noteworthy. She simply engages the serpent in debate.

The serpent begins by asking if God has specifically forbidden the man and the woman from eating any tree in the garden.

When Eve responds that she and the man will die if they sample fruit from the tree, the snake goads her on. "You will not die; for God knows that when you eat of it your eyes will be opened, and you will be like God."

▼ In *The Creation of Adam and Eve*, Isaak van Oosten depicts the creation of Adam (right), the creation of Eve out of Adam (center), to the eventual temptation (background). (17th century)

Adam and Eve, by an unknown artist, repeats a common misconception that Genesis identifies the forbidden fruit as an apple.

The serpent then contradicts what God has said and suggests that the command is part of a hidden agenda to deny Adam and Eve knowledge that has been reserved for God. God's reason for doing so, the serpent continues is not to protect Adam and Eve from death, as he claims, but to prevent them from becoming God's equals and possible rivals.

Since the fruit is appealing for food, delightful to look at, and has the added benefit of conferring wisdom, Eve eats it and gives it to Adam to taste as well. Immediately Adam and Eve's eyes are open.

THE FIRST CLOTHES

The first thing Adam and Eve focus on is their nakedness. Embarrassed, they sew fig leaves together to make clothes.

Later that day, when God is strolling in the garden, Adam and Eve conceal themselves. When God calls out to them, they say they are hiding because they are afraid of their nakedness.

God asks the humans who told them they were naked and accuses Adam and Eve of eating the forbidden fruit.

ADAM SHIFTS THE BLAME

Adam tries to shift the blame by saying it was the woman who gave him the fruit. Eve in turn implicates the serpent, explaining that it tricked her into tasting the fruit. God then turns to the serpent and places a curse on it, recorded in poetic form.

"Because you have done this, cursed are you among all animals and among all wild creatures; upon your belly you shall go,

16

Brueghel the Younger depicts God expelling Adam and Eve from paradise in *Expulsion From Eden.* (ca. 1624)

*and dust you shall eat
all the days of your life.
I will put enmity between you
and the woman,
and between your offspring and hers;
he will strike your head,
and you will strike his heel."*

God returns to Eve and curses her with pains in childbirth and submission to her husband. God tells Adam that because he followed Eve into sin, he has to work hard to make anything grow.

God also curses humans with death, saying, *"You are dust."*

PROFOUND IDEAS IN PACKED TEXT

The story of the Fall is a good example of how the Hebrew Bible packs some very large ideas into a fairly small amount of narrative text.

Genesis 3 manages to touch on each of these heavyweight philosophical issues:

- the origin of evil and its effect
- humans' eventual triumph over evil
- the relationship of woman to man
- the origin of pain in childbirth
- the reason for toil
- the origin of death
- the origin of clothes, and why we wear them
- the reason for humans' alienation from nature
- the source of humans' alienation from God
- the origin of sacrificial worship

And these are just a few.

The book of Genesis, especially the first four chapters, provides a framework for articulating some of the deepest questions we have as human beings, where we come from, why we are here, and how we relate to one another and God.

▲ Cain becomes jealous when God accepts Abel's sacrifice and not his in this lithograph by an unknown artist. (1880)

CAIN AND ABEL IN POPULAR CULTURE

The story of the rivalry between Cain and Abel recurs in books, films, and even psychology.

Literature: A core theme in novels like *Absalom, Absalom!* (William Faulkner), *East of Eden* (John Steinbeck), and *Kane and Abel* (Jeffrey Archer) is the conflict between brothers.

Film: *East of Eden* (adapted from the book) won an Academy Award. *Duel in the Sun*, about bad blood that runs between brothers Jesse and Lewt McCanles, was set in the old West.

Psychology: *The Cain Complex* is a psychological syndrome characterized by rivalry, competition, and extreme envy or jealousy of a sibling, leading to hatred.

▲ The theme of brothers fighting is central to the film *East of Eden* (1955). In this scene, the Trask brothers compete for the affections of a young woman.

GENESIS 4

Cain and Abel: The Start of Sibling Rivalry

GENESIS REVEALS THAT HUMAN CONFLICT IS AS OLD AS MANKIND.

The theme of alienation and loss that begins with the story of the Fall continues with Cain and Abel. Cain, the firstborn son of Eve, follows in his father's footsteps as a farmer. Abel, his younger brother, becomes a herdsman.

As the young men reach adulthood, both worship God by offering sacrifices. God receives Abel's offering from his flock. Cain's offering of produce or grain, however, is not well regarded.

Though God assures Cain that he will accept his offering if he does well, Cain is so jealous of Abel that he murders him.

When God confronts Cain and asks where Abel has gone, Cain famously replies, "Am I my brother's keeper?" God sentences Cain to wander the Earth, a punishment Cain fears will make others want to kill him.

To ensure his safety, God places a mark on Cain warning that anyone who murders him will suffer God's wrath.

The story of Cain and Abel sets the tone for much of what follows in the Hebrew Bible. The world is divided into "us" and "them." However, instead of rooting the seeds of rivalry in selfish ambition, the story of Cain and Abel involves God in the conflict. It is God's favor that they both seek, and it is God who advises Cain to try harder.

> **VERSE TO KNOW**
> "Then the Lord said to Cain, 'Where is your brother Abel?' he said, 'I do not know; am I my brother's keeper?'"
> **(Gen. 4:9)**

The Italian painter Tiziano Vecelli, known as Titian, shows the beginning of human violence in *Cain and Abel*. (1542)

▲ Cain builds a city and names it after his son, Enoch. By an unknown artist. (1900)

GENESIS 5

Adam and Eve's Connection to Noah

STORIES THAT FOLLOW THE LINEAGE OF THE FIRST HUMANS

Genesis 5 traces the bloodline of Seth, Adam and Eve's third son, to Noah—a much more thorough accounting than is offered for Cain's descendants. The discrepancy reflects the importance of Seth's lineage to the Hebrews.

While the genealogies in the Hebrew Bible contain few heroic tales, the personalities live extremely long lives, in the 700- to 800-year range. Among others, there is the warrior Lamech; Enoch, who doesn't die but is transported directly to God; and his son Methuselah, who lives to be 969 years old.

Genealogy Tree of Adam, from a print from *Arca Noe*, Amsterdam (1675)

▲ Fresco of Raphael's *Noah Building the Ark*, St. Peter's Basilica, Vatican City (15th century)

GENESIS 6–9

Starting Over: Noah and the Flood

GOD FINDS A RIGHTEOUS MAN TO RESTART THE HUMAN RACE AND ALL OF CREATION.

VERSE TO KNOW
". . . nor will I ever again destroy every living creature as I have done." (Gen. 8:21)

The flood narrative in Genesis 6–9, commonly referred to as the story of Noah's Ark, highlights God's goodness. While the rest of creation has become so wicked that it cannot be redeemed, God, to show mercy, chooses Noah to restart not only the human race but all of creation. The account also reveals a dark and troubling element: While God makes arrangements for Noah and his family to be saved, the rest of humanity perishes.

God gives Noah specific instructions for building an ark to preserve his family and a male and female of every land animal on Earth. Noah obeys and spends 100 years building the ark. Then when the rains begin, he gathers his family and the animals into the ark.

The torrential downpour lasts 40 days and 40 nights.

▶ The ark was made of cypress wood held together by pitch, a thick, dark substance obtained from distilling tars. It was 300 cubits (450 feet) long by 50 cubits (75 feet) wide by 30 cubits (45 feet) high. It had one upper and two lower decks, lots of rooms, a roof, a ramp, and a window.

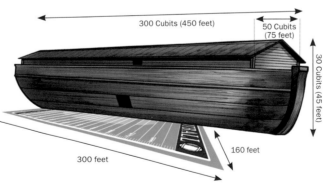

300 Cubits (450 feet)

50 Cubits (75 feet)

30 Cubits (45 feet)

300 feet

160 feet

▲ The dove returns, bringing an olive branch in Joaquin Ramirez's *The Interior of Noah's Ark.* (1857)

A PROMISE FROM GOD

After 150 days, the waters recede enough for the ark to land in the Ararat Mountains, in what is now modern-day Turkey. It is another 40 days before Noah is able to open a window, and the first thing he does is send out a series of birds to see if they can locate dry land.

When a dove returns to the ark with an olive branch in its mouth, Noah knows the waters have dried up enough that the ark's journey will soon be over.

After Noah determines that it is safe, he releases all of the animals.

The first thing Noah and his sons do is build an altar and send up offerings to God, who is pleased. God, in return, promises never to flood the entire Earth again. As a sign of his promise, God puts a rainbow in the sky.

Genesis says Noah's ark landed on "the mountains of Ararat," shown here in modern-day eastern Turkey.

▲ Engraving from *The Dove Bible* called *The Dove Sent Forth From the Ark* by French artist and illustrator Gustave Doré (1866)

Water Mark

Most geologists and archaeologists believe there is evidence of large-scale flooding in the Tigris–Euphrates basin. To the people who lived there in Biblical times, it would seem that the waters of the flood covered the world.

NEW EDEN? NOT FOR LONG . . .

God gives Noah's family a few rules to follow. If one person takes the life of another, the murderer should be executed. The clan is to have many children and take care of the land. And, in what is often considered the precursor to kosher dietary law, God allows Noah and his family to eat anything, plant or animal, but orders them to drain all the blood of an animal before cooking or consuming it.

NOAH'S STRANGE BEHAVIOR

Genesis 9:20-27 tells a strange story about drinking and cursing. After Noah settles down in the land, he plants grape vines, makes wine, and then ". . . became drunk, and he lay uncovered in his tent." Ham, Noah's youngest son, sees his father and calls his brothers to the tent. Taking care to avert their eyes, the three brothers work to cloak their father's naked form. When Noah wakes and discovers Ham has seen him undressed, he damns Canaan, Ham's son, with these words: "Cursed be Canaan; lowest of slaves shall he be to his brothers" (Gen. 9:25).

> **VERSE TO KNOW**
> "But Noah found favor in the eyes of the Lord." (Gen. 6:8)

There is no consensus on why Noah singles out Canaan, who was not involved in the dressing episode, instead of cursing Ham.

Some scholars speculate that editors included this section as a way to justify enslaving the Canaanites, the descendants of Canaan.

Whatever the reason for Noah's choice, it is clear for a second time that equality and peace on Earth have been interrupted for a second time.

Noah Cursing Canaan. This engraving depicts a common misconception—that Noah curses Ham. Instead, Noah focuses his anger on Ham's son, Canaan. (1754)

GENESIS 10–11
The Tower of Babel
CIVILIZATION IS BORN.

———————

After the great flood, mankind is united with new purpose. Noah's sons multiply, and all their children share the same customs and speak the same language. They spread out into surrounding lands and settle new kingdoms of their own. Noah's great-great-grandson, Nimrod, founds several cities in the land of Shinar, including the city of Babel. It is in Babel that the descendants of Noah decide to immortalize humanity's success by constructing a vast edifice, the Tower of Babel, with a top that reaches heaven itself.

God sees the work underway and decides to punish the Babylonians' pride. He curses humanity with new languages so that people can no longer communicate with one another and destroys unity in the land. The city is abandoned, and the Tower falls into ruin. The descendants of Noah now scatter farther abroad, to all corners of the Earth, and they take their new languages with them.

BABEL, BALAL, OR BABYLON?
"Babel" is the Hebrew name for the ancient city of Babylon. It's also very similar to the Hebrew word for "confusion," Balal, which is also used to describe the result of God's curse on the people of Babel. This play on words suggests the story might be metaphorical, but ancient Babylon was also home to multilayered pyramids called ziggurats. Some ziggurats were very tall and resembled towers. The great Temple of Marduk, a large ziggurat in ancient Babylon, may have inspired the story of the Tower of Babel.

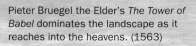

Pieter Bruegel the Elder's *The Tower of Babel* dominates the landscape as it reaches into the heavens. (1563)

The Sacrifice of Isaac by
Caravaggio (ca. 1603–1604)

CHAPTER 2

THE PROMISE OF A NATION

God calls Abram out of Mesopotamia, giving him a new name, Abraham, a new family, a new land, and makes him the first patriarch of the Hebrew people.

Built in 2000 B.C., the Tower of Ur with its 60-foot-high ziggurat Temple of the Chaldees was the capital of the Sumerian Dynasties in Iraq around the time of Abraham.

▲ Dating from the middle of the 3rd millennium B.C., "The Standard of Ur" is a Sumerian artifact found in a burial chamber near the ancestral homeland of Abraham in Ur, Iraq.

GENESIS 12

The Narrative Shifts to One Man and His Family

GOD AFFIRMS HIS COVENANT WITH HUMANITY
THROUGH HIS RELATIONSHIP WITH ABRAHAM.

Beginning with Genesis 12, the Bible's narrative moves from the world at large to the members of a single family: Here is the story of Abram, later to become Abraham, and his line of descendants.

As the chapter opens, God is promising to make Abram "a great nation." The story moves quickly to establish the passing of generations: Isaac, one of Abram's sons, produces two boys, Jacob and Esau, and each of those sons father a dozen male offspring of their own. Genesis first homes in on Jacob, who also has twelve sons, and then on Joseph, the second youngest and favorite son of Jacob.

In this telling, Abram's numerous male descendants are not a cohesive lot. The family members often are at odds with one another, and they rarely establish close relationships. In fact, a common story thread found in Genesis and throughout the Bible is the internecine strife between close relatives—a dynamic that is foreshadowed early on with the brother-versus-brother tale of Cain and Abel.

ABRAHAM: THE GREAT INFLUENCER

The story of Abraham is significant because it is deeply embedded in three important faith traditions.

Islam connects its heritage to Abraham's first son, Ishmael, and his descendants.

Judaism traces its patrimony through Abraham's second son, Isaac.

Christianity, while not claiming a biological connection to Abraham, does profess to be spiritually linked to his faith, particularly as it is expressed by his blood descendant, Jesus of Nazareth.

▲ *Angel Explaining to Abraham the Genealogy of Christ* by Ermengol of Beziers (late 13th–early 14th century)

Abram on His Journey to Canaan by Gustave Doré (19th century)

GENESIS 12

A Mission Revealed

GOD INSTRUCTS ABRAM TO LEAVE UR, JOURNEY
TO CANAAN, AND START A NEW NATION.

This chapter begins with a call and a promise from God to Abram, who is from Ur of the Chaldees. God's pledge consists of three parts:

- **A Land:** Abram is to leave his homeland and family and journey to a land that God will reveal to him.
- **A People:** God will make Abram a great name, and he will father a great nation to be a great blessing.
- **A Blessing:** Those who bless Abram will be blessed, and those who curse him will be cursed, and through Abram all the nations of the Earth will receive a blessing. Abram leaves the town of Haran,

where he is living, and with his wife Sarai, nephew Lot, and many relatives, he journeys south to Canaan.

As Abram reaches the ancient city of Shechem (near the modern West Bank town of Nablus), God identifies land that Abram's descendants will possess. Abram begins to build altars and offers sacrifices at strategic locations. Each altar represents a claim he is staking to the land for his posterity.

> "God identifies land that Abram's descendants will possess."

Abram is continuing south when famine strikes, and he detours to Egypt. Fearing the Egyptians will kill him and take Sarai, Abram tells his wife to pretend to be his sister. She agrees and joins Pharaoh's harem. To punish Pharaoh for taking Sarai, God afflicts the ruler with great plagues. Discovering Sarai's true identity, Pharaoh confronts Abram, who confesses, has Sarai returned to him, and goes north back into Canaan.

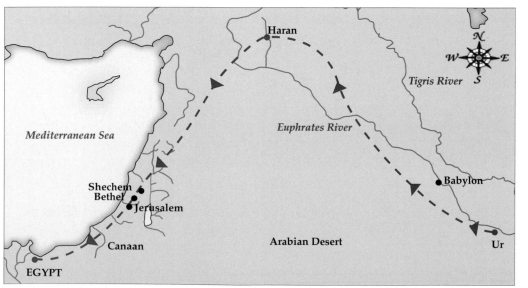

◀ The map traces Abram's journey from Ur up to Haran, then down to Canaan, and eventually to Egypt.

WHERE WAS UR?
Genesis identifies the city of Ur, also called Ur Kasdim, as Abraham's birthplace. Some have questioned if Ur was an actual city in Mesopotamia. Today, many scholars believe that the ruins of a massive temple complex near Nasiriya, Iraq, mark the site of the ancient Sumerian city of Ur.

GENESIS 16

Abram Produces Two Sons, but God Favors Isaac

ABRAM BECOMES ABRAHAM, AND EVENTUALLY, THE FATHER OF MANY.

Years pass, but Sarai does not conceive a child. She knows that for God's promise to be fulfilled and for Abram to father a great nation, her husband must produce an heir.

Sarai comes up with a plan. She persuades Abram to father a child with her young Egyptian slave, Hagar. The arrangement permits Sarai to keep her status as family matriarch and provides Abram a son through a surrogate.

Yet as Hagar's pregnancy progresses, the slave becomes increasingly contemptuous of Sarai. In turn, Sarai is so abusive of Hagar that she flees to the wilderness. There, Hagar is found by an angel who hears her complaints and persuades her to return and to submit to Sarai's authority. The angel promises Hagar that he will greatly multiply her offspring, but he warns that there will be perpetual strife between her son and all his kin.

Hagar is convinced and goes back to Sarai. She gives birth to Ishmael, whose name means "God has hearkened," in reference to God having heard her cries in the wilderness.

Thirteen years pass and Abram is now 99 years old. God appears to him again, this time in person, to renew and clarify his earlier promise that Abram will father a nation. God changes Abram's name to Abraham and Sarai's name to Sarah. He then says he will give the land of Canaan as a perpetual inheritance for Abram's descendants.

GOD ORDERS THE MEN TO BE CIRCUMCISED
God then establishes male circumcision as the sign that Abraham's descendants will inherit Canaan as promised. He also states that Sarah will be the mother of a son whose name will be Isaac and who will inherit the everlasting covenant. Abraham pleads on behalf of Ishmael, and God provides him a blessing as well.

Though Abraham is skeptical of God's orders, he follows through with the instructions and has all the males in his household circumcised. This establishes a custom that persists to this day among Jews, Muslims, and many Christians.

▼ *Hagar Introduced to Abraham* by Victor Orsel (18th century)

The Mexican painter José Salomé Pina depicts a pitiful scene in *Hagar and Ishmael Sent Away from the House of Abraham*. (1852)

▲ Italian painter Gaudenzio Ferrari portrays Abraham serving food to his guests in *Abraham and the Three Angels*. (16th century)

GENESIS 18

Weeding Out the Wicked

ABRAHAM WARNS THAT SODOM AND GOMORRAH WILL BE DESTROYED.

Genesis 18 begins some time later with the appearance of three men whom Abraham perceives to be divine. The visitors reiterate God's promise that Sarah will soon bear a son, and Sarah, overhearing their conversation, laughs at the idea since she is now advanced in years and unlikely to conceive. The visitors remark on Sarah laughing at the promise, although she denies it.

After feasting, Abraham accompanies two of the men safely on their way. One, identified in the text as Yahweh, stays behind to discuss with Abraham the fate of two wicked cities, Sodom and Gomorrah. Yahweh tells his host that the towns are so corrupt they must be destroyed.

Worried that innocent lives will be lost, Abraham asks whether the cities can be spared if righteous souls can be found. Yahweh agrees to the proposal and Abraham returns to his tent.

LOT'S WIFE LOOKS BACK

Arriving in Sodom, Abraham's former visitors warn Lot, Abraham's nephew, that destruction is coming. They urge him to gather his extended family and leave the kingdom without looking back. Lot is able to convince only his wife and two daughters to flee. As they depart, Lot's wife lingers for a last glimpse and is turned into a pillar of salt as a firestorm of burning sulfur descends.

The destruction so traumatizes Lot that he abandons his plans to live in the nearby town of Zoar and instead takes his daughters to live in the open countryside. The family moves into a cave, which the daughters believe will ruin their prospects for marriage and condemn them to end their days as spinster beggars. To avoid that fate, the sisters each get their father drunk and sleep with him. The oldest daughter conceives a male child she names Moab or "the seed of the father." The younger daughter produces a son she names Ben-ammi, or "son of my kindred." These brothers become founders of the tribal nations of Moab and Ammon, which figure prominently in the later history of Israel.

> "As they depart, Lot's wife lingers for a last glimpse and is turned into a pillar of salt . . ."

▲ In *The Destruction of Sodom and Gomorrah*, John Martin portrays the fire that engulfs both cities. (1852)

VERSE TO KNOW

"Shall I indeed bear a child, now that I am old?" (Gen. 18:13)

The Dome of the Rock in Jerusalem sits atop the place on Mount Moriah where Abraham is thought to have attempted to sacrifice Isaac.

VALUABLE ASSETS

Goats, sheep, and other livestock in Biblical times are among the most valuable assets people own, and animals are sacrificed to signify important or solemn occasions such as weddings, funerals, and births.

Animal sacrifice also highlights the reverence and respect that people have for the meat they put on the table.

▲ *Ariete* by Francisco de Zurbaran (17th century)

GENESIS 21

A Son Named Isaac

SARAH FINALLY CONCEIVES
A CHILD FOR ABRAHAM.

As God has promised, Sarah, who is 90, gives birth to a son and she names him Isaac, meaning "laughter." To prevent a rivalry with Ishmael, Sarah insists that Abraham send Hagar and her son away. Abraham is reluctant. He loves Ishmael and only agrees to banish his firstborn after an angel arrives and promises that Ishmael also will be the father of a great nation. Ishmael goes on to father 12 sons who become 12 tribal nations. Hagar gets lost in the wilderness but then is rescued from starvation by an angel.

The worst is not over for Abraham, who must now face the most severe test of his faith and willingness to obey all of God's commands. God instructs the aging patriarch to take Isaac, his promised heir, and to sacrifice him on the top of Mount Moriah. Abraham, with his mature faith in God, sets out with his son to comply. When Isaac asks why they have made all the necessary preparations for a sacrifice but have no animal to offer, Abraham replies, "God himself will provide the lamb for a burnt offering, my son." **(Genesis 22:8)**

The narrative describes Abraham building the altar, ordering the wood on it, and then placing Isaac atop the pile. However, just as Abraham is about to plunge his knife into the boy's body, an angel stops his hand, and God points to a ram that is caught in the thicket of nearby bushes. The father and son are able to make a sacrifice of the ram.

An angel stops Abraham just in time in *The Sacrifice of Isaac* by Laurent de la Hyre. (17th century)

▲ Italian painter Gregorio Lazzarini shows Isaac's future wife meeting Abraham's servant Eliezer in *Rebecca and Eliezer.* (ca. 1705)

Arranging a Marriage

ABRAHAM SENDS ISAAC TO THEIR HOMELAND TO FIND A WIFE.

When Isaac is 37, Sarah passes away and Abraham decides it is time for Isaac to marry. He sends his son to their ancestral homeland to find a member of the family to take as a bride.

The caravan heads north and arrives at a well. One of Abraham's servants, hesitant to trust his own judgment, asks God for help. He wonders if the first woman who offers to provide water for him and his 10 camels can be Isaac's bride. While the servant is praying, a young woman shows up at the well and draws a jar of water. The servant asks her for a drink, and she readily offers her jar to him.

The woman then suggests she also can give water to his camels until their thirst is satisfied, and she returns to the well to refill her water jar.

The servant is delighted with such an obvious answer to his prayer and inquires

Isaac and Rebecca's Wedding Feast by an unknown artist (17th century)

MEETING AT THE WELL

In pastoral cultures, where life is impossible without a reliable source of water, wells are valuable family assets that are passed down through the generations. To prevent conflict over water rights, elaborate hospitality customs evolve to balance the needs of itinerant strangers and the well's owners.

Wells are gathering places where shepherds watering their flocks exchange news with passing caravans and where local women congregate daily, usually in the cool morning, to draw water for the household needs. Given the central role wells play in the culture, it is logical that Abraham's servant chooses to start his search for Isaac's wife at a watering hole.

▲ Isaac encounters Rebekah at a well like this one.

about the woman's parentage. He discovers she is indeed a close relative of Abraham, and he offers her a gold nose ring and gold bracelets. He asks to be taken to meet her father, and the young woman, named Rebekah, agrees.

On the way home, Rebekah encounters her brother Laban, who notices the new jewelry. Rebekah shares her story, and Laban immediately ushers the servant and the rest of Abraham's caravan to their camp so they can clean up from their journey, rest, and eat.

The servant explains that the group is on a mission to find a wife for Isaac, and that Rebekah is the answer to his prayer at the well. He then asks if Laban is willing to proceed with marriage arrangements for his sister right away.

Laban agrees, Isaac marries Rebekah and is comforted after his mother's death, and the caravan returns to Canaan.

Italian Baroque painter Bernardo Strozzi portrays Jacob tricking his father in *Isaac Blessing Jacob*. (ca. 1625)

GENESIS 25

A Rivalry Is Born

GOD TELLS REBEKAH THAT HER YOUNGER SON
JACOB WILL SUPPLANT HIS OLDER BROTHER ESAU.

Like Sarah, Rebekah remains childless for many years of marriage. She finally conceives twins after Isaac prays on her behalf, but the babies struggle with each other even in the womb. Rebekah asks God why this is, and he explains that she has two nations inside of her fighting for dominance and that the elder will serve the younger.

This notion carries over into the names of the boys when they are born. The elder son, who is red and covered with hair, is dubbed Esau, or "hairy." The younger son, who grips the heel of his older brother as he enters the world, is named Jacob, which translates as "supplanter."

Genesis summarizes Esau's character in an episode in which he returns empty-handed from a hunting expedition. Famished, Esau comes upon Jacob cooking a pot of stew and asks to eat. Jacob agrees,

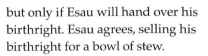

The tender moment when the two brothers reunite is captured in Italian painter Francesco Hayez's *Meeting of Jacob and Esau*. (1844)

but only if Esau will hand over his birthright. Esau agrees, selling his birthright for a bowl of stew.

Years later when Isaac lays dying, Jacob tricks Esau again, this time with Rebekah's help. Mother and son convince Isaac that the person serving him his final meal is Esau when it is really Jacob. Isaac unwittingly confers his blessing on Jacob, the younger son, making him the family patriarch. He utters: "Be lord over your brothers, and may your mother's sons bow down to you. Cursed be everyone who curses you, and blessed be everyone who blesses you."

Esau also gets a blessing from Isaac, but he is now so filled with hatred for his brother, he plots to murder him. As Isaac is dying, he instructs Jacob to return to the family's ancestral homeland to find a wife, effectively removing Jacob from Esau's murderous reach.

Jacob sees angels climbing a ladder up to heaven in *Jacob's Dream*, a work by Italian Baroque painter Domenico Fetti. (ca. 1620)

GENESIS 32
Double Crossed by Laban

JACOB SEEKS TO MARRY RACHEL AND ENDS UP WITH TWO WIVES.

One night on the way back to his ancestral homeland, Jacob stops to sleep. He dreams of a ladder rising to heaven with angels who climb up and down the rungs. God speaks to Jacob, reaffirming the gift of land he promised Abraham and Isaac.

On awaking, Jacob names the place where he has slept Bethel ("House of God") and vows that if God protects him on his journey, he will take God as his Lord and will give a tenth of all that he earns back to God.

When Jacob arrives in the territory of his ancestors, he stops at a well and asks if any of the shepherds know of Laban in Haran. Just then, Laban's beautiful daughter Rachel arrives with a flock of sheep. Jacob rolls away the stone that is covering the well and waters her flocks. Then he greets her with a kiss and tells her that he is Rebekah's son. She runs home and tells Laban who greets Jacob enthusiastically and houses him for a month.

Laban notices Jacob is working for him without pay. He asks Jacob what he wants in compensation for his labor. Jacob asks for his daughter Rachel. The two men agree that Jacob will work for Laban for seven years, and in exchange, Jacob will receive Rachel as his wife.

At the end of the seven years, Laban hosts a huge wedding. However, instead of presenting Jacob with Rachel, he substitutes her older sister, Leah. The next morning, Jacob

In *Jacob Meeting Rachel*, Austrian painter Joseph von Fuhrich portrays the couple's first encounter. (1836)

Jacob Wrestles with an Angel by Edward Jakob von Steinle (19th century)

discovers the deception and confronts Laban, who says it is not customary for the younger sister to marry before the older one. Laban offers to give Rachel to Jacob only after another seven years of labor, and Jacob assents.

Six years pass and Jacob has become independently wealthy. He senses that his riches are making Laban's field hands jealous, and he hastily arranges to leave Haran, taking Rachel and Leah with him. When Laban learns that Jacob has fled, he pursues and demands an explanation from his son-in-law.

Jacob struggles with what to do, both during his waking hours and while he sleeps, when God sends and an angel to wrestle with him. Neither Jacob nor the angel are able to gain an advantage in the fight

> "Laban's beautiful daughter Rachel arrives with a flock of sheep."

until the angel strikes Jacob in the hip socket. It is a blow that leaves Jacob lame for the rest of his life, but Jacob clings tenaciously to the angel and says, "I will not let you go unless you bless me." **(Genesis 32:26)** The angel consents and changes his name from Jacob ("supplanter") to Israel ("Prince of God").

Jacob releases the angel and continues south to Canaan to face Esau. Jacob approaches his brother cautiously and the meeting goes well.

Brothers Sell Joseph into Slavery by Russian painter Konstantin Flavitsky (ca. 1860)

GENESIS 37

Joseph Becomes a Slave in Egypt

JACOB'S FAVORITE SON IS TOSSED INTO A PIT BY HIS BROTHERS AND LEFT FOR DEAD.

Between his two wives and two concubines, Jacob now has 11 sons, but they are so unruly and hateful that Jacob is forced to move the family from Shechem south to Bethel.

He continues a semi-nomadic existence for years, moving often from one location to another. During one such transfer, Rachel, his favorite wife, dies while giving birth to Jacob's youngest son, named Benjamin.

Because Jacob loved Rachel dearly, he treats Joseph, the second youngest son, the best. He designs a special coat for him as a sign of his approval, alienating his other sons. Joseph creates even more conflict by relating symbolic dreams that suggest his brothers will bow down to him. The brothers consider Joseph ambitious and a potential threat and plot to kill him.

They first agree to slay Joseph when he comes searching for them out in the fields with the livestock. But the oldest brother, Reuben, persuades his siblings to instead sell Joseph into slavery and to make it look like an accidental death.

The 11 brothers strip Joseph of his robe and toss him into a pit. Then they rip the garment into pieces, cover it in blood, and present it to their father. Joseph is discovered by nomadic merchants, who sell him as a slave to men in a caravan headed south to Egypt. Joseph's brothers don't know Joseph's fate.

Joseph's brothers show Jacob the coat of many colors to prove that Joseph is dead in this work by an unknown artist (1855)

Mexican painter Juan Urruchi portrays Potiphar's wife attempting to seduce Joseph in *Joseph and Potiphar's Wife*. (1852)

GENESIS 39–41

A Slave Triumphs

JOSEPH INTERPRETS PHARAOH'S
DREAMS AND SAVES EGYPT.

THE INTERPRETATION OF DREAMS

The ancients clearly distinguish between "everyday" dreams and those of a prophetic nature.

Joseph's brothers may mock him and call him "Dreamer," but they recognize the significance of his visions and the need to put a stop to them before they came true.

Jacob, having had a prophetic dream of his own, ponders the meaning of Joseph's dreams more deeply than his sons do.

In Egypt, Joseph is sold into the household of Potiphar, an officer in Pharaoh's guard. Joseph advances within the household but is thrown into prison after Potiphar's wife unfairly accuses him of attempting to violate her.

Joseph begins interpreting the dreams of the Pharaoh's ex-chief baker and ex-chief cupbearer and becomes a valued figure in the prison. The men agree to mention Joseph to Pharaoh after they are released. However, when the cupbearer gets his job back, he forgets about Joseph. It is only two years later, when Pharaoh has some bad dreams, that Joseph is summoned and hears what Pharaoh has seen at night.

In the first dream, Pharaoh is standing by the Nile when seven fat cows come out of

the water and begin eating the grass along the riverbank. Then seven thin cows come out of the river and eat the fat cows, but even after devouring them, the thin cows remain thin.

In the second dream, Pharaoh sees seven fat ears of grain growing on a stalk, waving in the wind. Then, seven thin, blighted ears of corn sprout and consume the fat ears.

Joseph explains that Egypt will face seven years of abundance followed by seven years of famine. Joseph recommends that Pharaoh appoint an administrator to oversee emergency preparations and to stockpile grain.

Pharaoh names Joseph overseer and gives him broad administrative powers to implement the plan that he proposes.

▲ *Joseph of Egypt in Prison* by German Bohemian painter Anton Raphael Mengs (18th century)

Joseph Forgiving His Brothers for Selling Him into Slavery by an unknown artist (20th century)

GENESIS 42–49

Joseph's Revenge and Reconciliation

DESPITE EVERYTHING, HE FORGIVES HIS BROTHERS AND IS REUNITED WITH HIS FAMILY.

Events transpire exactly as Joseph predicts and when the famine comes, Egypt, with its stockpiles of grain, thrives while its neighbors suffer. Nearby in Canaan, Jacob hears rumors that the Egyptians have food. Hoping to purchase some for his family, Jacob dispatches his 10 eldest sons to the south, while keeping Benjamin at home.

The brothers reach Egypt and arrange to meet the government official in charge of the grain. That administrator is Joseph, but 13 years have passed and the brothers don't recognize the 30-year old. They prostrate themselves before him, begging for grain. Joseph remembers his boyhood dream where his brothers bowed to him and decides to teach them a lesson.

In asking for Joseph's kindness, the brothers mention they have left their youngest member at home. Joseph accuses his siblings of being spies and demands proof that their story is true. He announces he will keep all 10 in prison until someone travels to Canaan and brings the young boy to Egypt. After locking the brothers up for three days, Joseph brings them out.

Joseph speaks in Egyptian and uses a translator to communicate with his brothers who still don't realize who he is. But talking among themselves, the brothers agree they are being punished for how they treated Joseph many years ago. At this sign of remorse, Joseph turns away weeping. He releases nine of the brothers and tells them to return home to fetch Benjamin, their youngest. Joseph secretly returns the money the brothers paid to the grain sacks and keeps the 10th brother, Simeon, in jail.

Arriving home, the brothers convince Jacob to allow Benjamin to return with them to see the administrator, and set off for Egypt. But Joseph is not done with his tricks. This time, he hides a silver cup among Benjamin's possessions, and the

JOSEPH AND FORGIVENESS—A MODEL FOR RECONCILIATION?

The story of Joseph forgiving his brothers is touching but seems out of place in Genesis, a book filled with retribution. Joseph's brothers commit a terrible wrong against him and then lie about it to their father. Joseph spends years in prison because of them. He would be justified to use his power to exact revenge upon them. But he doesn't. He gives them what they don't give him—mercy.

ALL IN THE FAMILY

The 12 tribes of Israel, each with their own land, are based on Jacob's sons. Joseph gets two tribes, and the others each get one except Levi, whose descendants live in cities and become priests and temple functionaries.

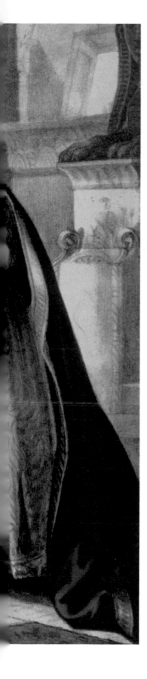

boy is accused of theft. Joseph announces that in punishment, Benjamin must serve as his slave.

JOSEPH FORGIVES HIS BROTHERS

Judah, the fourth eldest, pleads with Joseph to release Benjamin and offers to serve as the slave instead. Joseph breaks down at this sign of self-sacrifice and reveals that he is their brother. He says he is not angry and that all the events were orchestrated by God to save them from starvation. He sends the brothers to retrieve their father, Jacob, and the rest of their families to live in Egypt for the duration of the famine.

Before Jacob dies, he declares that his 12 sons will inherit the house of Israel. He includes Joseph's sons Ephraim and Manasseh in this blessing, effectively doubling Joseph's inheritance at the expense of his brothers.

▲ *Jacob Blessing Joseph's Sons* by Rembrandt (1656)

VERSE TO KNOW

"I am your brother, Joseph, whom you sold into Egypt." (Gen. 45:4)

CHAPTER 3

JOURNEY TO THE PROMISED LAND

Exodus, one of the Bible's most significant books, chronicles the liberation of the Hebrews from Egypt, Moses's acceptance of the Ten Commandments, and the establishment of Canaan as their homeland. Moses and his brother, Aaron, seek to follow God's instructions and lead the restless, often unhappy and rebellious Hebrews to the promised land.

▲ Moses leads the Hebrews out of slavery into the wilderness of Sinai in this hand-colored woodcut. (19th century)

WHICH PHAROAH?
Scholars across many disciplines have attempted to identify the Egyptian Pharaoh encountered by Moses and Aaron in Exodus. Here are some candidates:

- Ahmose I
  (1550–1525 B.C.)
- Thutmose III
  (1479–1425 B.C.)
- Horemheb
  (1319–1292 B.C.)
- Ramesses I
  (1292–1290 B.C.)
- Ramesses II
  (1279–1213 B.C.)

EXODUS 1 & 2

A Hebrew Slave is Raised As a Prince of Egypt

DISCOVERING HIS FATE, MOSES
BECOMES A FUGITIVE.

As Exodus opens, it is the worst possible time to be a Hebrew in Egypt. The people are slaves and have been for hundreds of years. They are mistreated, forced by the Egyptians to build cities and monuments by hand. Pharaoh, Egypt's leader, fears the population is growing too quickly and that it will rebel. To prevent an uprising, he issues a strict command to his people:

"Every boy that is born to the Hebrews you shall throw into the Nile."

The Hebrew Jochebed, who has just given birth to Moses, defies Pharaoh's command. For three months, she keeps the infant's birth a secret. But as Moses grows, Jochebed knows it will be difficult to hide him forever. She puts Moses in a basket and leaves him in the Nile River. There, the infant is found by the Pharaoh's daughter, who takes him to the palace.

Although Moses grows up as a privileged member of the royal family, he knows he is adopted and begins to suspect that he was born a Hebrew,

> **WHAT'S IN A NAME?**
> In Hebrew, the word *Moses* sounds like the phrase for "draw out."

not an Egyptian. At the palace, Moses hears rumors about the way the Hebrews are being mistreated, and when he turns 40, decides to discover the truth for himself.

One day, while out walking, Moses is horrified to see an Egyptian overlord beating a Hebrew slave. He jumps to the worker's defense, attacking and killing the

Egyptian. Moses hides the man's body in the sand and assumes the worker will be grateful for the aid. But an incident the next day makes it clear that the slave did not understand where Moses's sympathies lie.

Out again on the streets of Egypt, Moses comes across a Hebrew mistreating a man. He calls out to the aggressor,

"Why do you strike your fellow Hebrew?"

The man replies,

"Who made you a ruler and judge over us? Do you mean to kill me as you killed the Egyptian?"

Moses is terrified that word of the murder has spread and that Pharaoh will send soldiers to arrest him. He decides to flee and sets out for the land of Midian, several hundred miles away on the other side of the Sinai Peninsula. In a short time, Moses has gone from being a prince of Egypt to a fugitive far from home.

▲ Pharaoh's daughter discovers an infant in a basket floating along the Nile in Nicolas Poussin's *The Finding of Moses* (1651).

▲ *Moses Defending the Daughters of Jethro* by Charles Le Brun (1687)

EXPLORING THE MEANING OF THE NAMES FOR GOD

- **I am that I am** or **I am**. This name signifies various aspects of God's identity. (1) God is self-existent; (2) He is eternal and unchangeable; (3) He is incomprehensible; (4) He is true to his promises.

- **The Lord (Yahweh).** When the name "the Lord" appears in small caps in the Old Testament, it refers to the four-letter Hebrew word pronounced "Yahweh." It means "He is" or "He will be." This holy name for God was so revered by the Jewish people that in later years the Jewish people were afraid to speak it.

EXODUS 3–6

Called to Lead

MOSES FINDS A WIFE, MEETS GOD, AND RETURNS TO EGYPT TO CONFRONT PHARAOH.

Moses arrives in Midian and stops at a well where seven sisters, the daughters of a priest, are watering their flock. Soon shepherds appear with their own thirsty sheep. When the men try to chase the sisters away, Moses intervenes and the shepherds retreat.

In gratitude, the sisters invite Moses to meet their father, the priest Jethro, who offers the stranger a job as a shepherd. Soon, Moses joins the family by marrying one of the sisters, Zipporah.

Forty years pass. Moses, now 80, is with his sheep on the far side of Mt. Horeb. Suddenly, he is startled by a bush that appears to be burning. It is an angel of the Lord. As Moses draws closer to the bush, he hears God call to him. God identifies himself:

"I am the God of your father, the God of Abraham, the God of Isaac, and the God of Jacob. I have observed the misery of my people who are in Egypt. . . . I have come down . . . to bring them up out of that land to . . . a land flowing with milk and honey."

God tells Moses that he must return to Egypt to lead the Hebrews out of bondage. Moses protests that he is ill for such a task, and in response, God bestows upon him a set of miraculous powers. Moses is now

able to turn a staff into a snake and make his own hand leprous. These signs of God's might are to serve as a warning to Pharaoh to free the Hebrews or risk calamity for his own people.

Moses remains reluctant, and God decides that Aaron, Moses's brother, should also travel to Egypt to confront Pharaoh.

Once the brothers arrive at the palace and meet with Pharaoh, they both tell him that the God of Israel says,

"Let my people go."

Pharaoh replies,

"Who is the Lord, that I should heed him and let Israel go?"

To underscore his power, Pharaoh orders the slave masters to stop giving the Hebrews straw for brick-making, which makes it impossible for the workers to meet their quotas, but the Egyptians begin demanding even more bricks and beat the Hebrews' overseers. In despair, the overseers protest to Pharaoh, who tells them they are lazy and orders them back to work.

The overseers protest to Moses and Aaron, and Moses goes to the Lord for answers. God tells him, *Now you shall see what I will do to Pharaoh.*

Pharaoh is unaware of the wrath that is about to descend on him and all of Egypt.

▲ Raphael's *Moses and the Burning Bush* from the loggia at the Hermitage Museum, St. Petersburg, Russia (1513)

VERSE TO KNOW

"The Lord said to [Moses], . . . 'Now go, and I will be with your mouth and teach you what you are to speak.'" (Exodus 4:12)

▲ Moses lifts his staff to call down another plague in John Martin's *One of the Seven Plagues of Egypt.* (1754)

THE PASSOVER HOLIDAY
To help remember how God delivers them from the Egyptians, the Israelites begin to celebrate the Passover feast every year on the 14th of the month of Nisan. During that week, the Hebrews refrain from all work except food preparation.

VERSE TO KNOW
"Sing to the Lord, for he has triumphed gloriously; horse and rider he has thrown into the sea." (**Exodus 15:21**)

EXODUS 6–15

Plagues, Passover, and the Exodus

MOSES AND AARON FACE PHARAOH
IN AN EPIC BATTLE OF WILLS.

Pharaoh continues to doubt God's powers, forcing Moses and Aaron to use their staff to turn the water in the Nile—in streams, ponds, and even water buckets—to blood. The first plague kills the river fish, and their rotting smell spreads. Pharaoh refuses to believe that the Hebrew God is responsible for the horror and denies the people passage out of Egypt.

Seven days later, Pharaoh again rebuffs Moses and Aaron's demand to free the Hebrews. For the second plague, God instructs Moses to hold his staff out over the Nile. When he does, hordes of frogs fill the river and hop up onto the land.

Pharaoh tells Moses that if he gets rid of the frogs, he will let the Hebrews go. But once the frogs vanish, Pharaoh reneges on his promise.

Eight more plagues are visited upon the Egyptians. After the ninth, Pharaoh is so overwhelmed, he banishes Moses from Egypt, telling him:

"Get away from me! Take care that you do not see my face again, for on the day you see my face you shall die."

WORST PLAGUE OF ALL
When Pharaoh again refuses to let the Hebrews go, God unleashes a final, horrific plague: He calls for the slaying of all first-born Egyptian males.

The curse is so terrible that God gives Moses special instructions to prepare for it. Each Hebrew household is told to take a one-year-old male lamb or goat without defects and on the 14th day of the month, to kill, roast, and eat it. In order to be "passed over" and spared, they are to use the animal's

At Moses's order, the waters of the Red Sea come together to cover Pharaoh's army in this work by an unknown artist. (ca. 1900)

blood to mark the top and sides of their doorposts.

On the night of the 10th plague, the Hebrews follow all the instructions. They come to the table dressed and ready to travel. They eat in haste and wait for the Lord's command to leave Egypt.

At midnight, the 10th plague kills all the firstborn Egyptian males in Egypt. Not even the firstborn livestock are spared. Exodus 12 records that all over Egypt loud crying and wailing could be heard as firstborn males died.

THE HEBREWS LEAVE EGYPT

During the night, Pharaoh summons Moses and Aaron and orders all the Hebrews out of Egypt where they have lived for 430 years.

As the people leave, Pharaoh changes his mind again and sends soldiers after them. When the Hebrews are camping at the edge

of the Red Sea, they spot the Egyptian warriors approaching and panic because they have no escape route. Moses tells them not to fear.

A cloud the Hebrews have been following moves so that it separates them from the Egyptians. Throughout the night, the cloud shrouds the soldiers in darkness and provides light for the people.

Then Moses stretches out his hand over the Red Sea, and a pathway through the water opens up. The Israelites hurry through the divided waters to dry ground on the opposite bank. The Egyptians follow in their chariots, and God gives Moses a command.

"Stretch out your hand over the sea, so that the water may come back upon the Egyptians."

Moses lifts up his arm, and the Red Sea closes over the Egyptian soldiers. The Israelites escape their captors and are finally free. But their journey has just begun.

> **"During the night, Pharaoh summons Moses and Aaron and orders all the Hebrews out of Egypt . . ."**

THE 10 PLAGUES

Water to Blood
The water throughout Egypt is turned to blood. The fish die and rot, and a stench fills the land.

Frogs
Egypt is overrun with frogs, which swarm the rivers, the royal palace, and even Pharaoh's bedchamber.

Gnats
All the dust of the earth turns to gnats, which descend on men and animals alike.

Flies
Multitudes of flies invade the homes of the Egyptian people. The land is ruined.

Diseased Livestock
A pestilence strikes and kills horses, donkeys, camels, sheep, and goats.

Boils
As Moses throws soot into the air, painful boils appear on humans and animals.

Thunder and Hail
A horrible hailstorm kills people, livestock, and crops.

Locusts
A swarm of locusts covers the sky and eats what's left of the Egyptians' crops.

Darkness
Three days without sunlight prevent Egyptians from working and moving about.

Death of the Firstborn
The worst plague of all kills all of Egypt's firstborn sons, including male livestock.

Moses destroys the sacred tablets after seeing the Israelites worshiping the golden calf, by an unknown artist.

"If you obey my voice . . . you shall be my treasured possession out of all the peoples." (Exodus 19:5)

EXODUS 19-31

Receiving the Law

GOD GIVES MOSES THE TEN COMMANDMENTS.

After three months of travel, the Israelites arrive at Mount Sinai, where God tells Moses that he will make the Hebrews his chosen people if they obey his commandments and keep his covenant.

Three days later, a thick cloud covers Mount Sinai. Thunder rumbles and lightning flashes. A sudden blast from a trumpet startles everyone. In a blaze of light, the Lord begins to announce his commandments, but the sound of his voice so upsets the Hebrews that they beg Moses to receive God's orders alone. The people agree they will follow all of the Lord's instructions, and Moses sets off on his mission.

At the top of Mount Sinai, Moses meets with God and receives the Ten Commandments, which are chiseled into stone tablets. He remains there for 40 days and nights, learning how God expects the people to worship and conduct themselves.

Uncertain why Moses is taking so long, the Hebrews go to Aaron and ask him to make golden idols for them to worship. Aaron agrees and casts gold into the shape of a calf. Aaron announces a ceremony for the next day. At the festival, the people worship the golden calf.

God observes the Hebrews and orders Moses down the mountain. Carrying the tablets, Moses begins the long descent. When he arrives at the camp and sees the people dancing around the glittery statue, Moses smashes the panels in anger.

▲ *The Adoration of the Golden Calf* from the loggia of Raphael, Hermitage Museum, St. Petersburg, Russia

God tells Moses to climb back up Mount Sinai, so he can write the Ten Commandments on two new stone tablets.

The Hebrews stay at Mount Sinai for several more months. During this time, God gives Moses instructions for workers to build a special case, or Ark of the Covenant, to hold the Ten Commandments. God also orders the construction of a home for the Ark, which he calls the tabernacle.

THE TEN COMMANDMENTS, AGAIN

In 1956, Paramount Pictures released *The Ten Commandments*. This was director Cecil B. DeMille's second movie of the same title. The first, released in 1923, was a silent movie. The 1956 release, shot on location in Egypt, was based on the Bible, archeology, and historical writings. It was nominated for seven Academy Awards and won for Best Visual Effects.

WRITTEN IN STONE

1. "I am the Lord your God, who brought you out of Egypt, out of the house of slavery. You shall have no other gods before me." (Exodus 20:2, 3)

2. "You shall not make for yourself an idol, whether in the form of anything that is in heaven above, or that is on the earth beneath, or that is in the water under the earth. You shall not bow down to them or worship them" (Exodus 20:4, 5)

3. "You shall not make wrongful use of the name of the Lord your God, for the Lord will not acquit anyone who misuses his name." (Exodus 20:7)

4. "Remember the sabbath day, and keep it holy. Six days you shall labor and do all your work. But the seventh day is a sabbath to the Lord your God; you shall not do any work" (Exodus 20:8–10)

5. "Honor your father and your mother, so that your days may be long in the land that the Lord your God is giving you." (Exodus 20:12)

6. "You shall not murder." (Exodus 20:13)

7. "You shall not commit adultery." (Exodus 20:14)

8. "You shall not steal." (Exodus 20:15)

9. "You shall not bear false witness against your neighbor." (Exodus 20:16)

10. "You shall not covet your neighbor's wife." (Exodus 20:17)

Joshua and Caleb return to Canaan loaded with grapes, by an unknown artist (1880)

The Brazen Serpent, by an unknown artist, depicts the healing of Israelites bitten by snakes.

VERSE TO KNOW

"The Lord bless you and keep you; the Lord make his face to shine upon you, and be gracious to you; the Lord lift up his countenance upon you, and give you peace."
(Numbers 6:24-26)

LEVITICUS

Leviticus is the third book of the Torah. It provides Hebrews with laws that make them the chosen people, and addresses the form of sacrificial rites, cleanliness, the actions of priests, and moral behavior. Leviticus outlines kosher dietary rules and Israel's sacred holidays, including Passover, which celebrates the exodus from Egypt and the receiving of the Torah, and the Day of Atonement, the holiest day of the year, in which the people are to fast and self-reflect.

NUMBERS 1–14, DEUTERONOMY

Spy Trip, Rebellion

THE HEBREWS PREPARE TO ENTER THE PROMISED LAND.

God orders a census of his people and divides the Hebrews into 12 tribes based on ancestral families. The tribes are named after the 12 sons of Jacob, with two exceptions. The Levites are excluded from the count and instead are assigned the task of caring for the tabernacle and assisting with sacrifices. Similarly, God does not create a tribe named after Joseph, since Jacob adopted Joseph's two sons (Ephraim and Manasseh) as his own.

While the Hebrews camp in the Desert of Paran, the Lord tells Moses to send some men to explore Canaan. Moses selects one leader from each tribe for the expedition and asks them to bring back

VERSE TO KNOW
"Hear, O Israel: The Lord is our God, the Lord alone."
(Deuteronomy 6:4)

reports about the land, the people, and the towns.

Over the next 40 days, the men investigate Canaan and return to Moses reporting that the land is flowing with milk and honey.

Yet chaos ensues. One of the spies, Caleb, urges an immediate attack. The other men

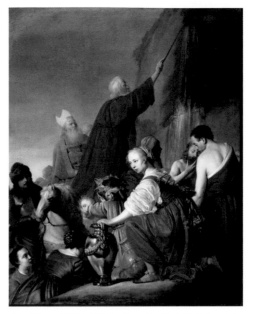

▲ In *Moses Striking Water from the Rock*, Dutch painter Salomon de Coninck portrays Moses losing control to bring forth water in this 17th century painting.

sentences them to wander the desert for the next 40 years.

FOR MANY, DEATH BY SNAKE BITE

At times, the people lose hope, fret, and rebel. The unrest offends God, and on one occasion, he sends venomous snakes into the camp where the Hebrews are staying. When many die of bite wounds, Moses asks God to remove the serpents. God tells Moses to make a model of a snake, put it on a pole, and walk through the camp. Whoever has been bitten and sees the pole will live.

Later, when the Hebrews reach Kadesh and water runs low, they complain to Moses again. Frustrated, Moses calls out, "Listen, you rebels, shall we bring water for you out of this rock?" **(Numbers 20:10)**

Though God has instructed Moses to speak to the rock, he instead hits it twice with his staff and water gushes out. This act of disobedience angers God, who punishes Moses. Now, Joshua, not Moses and Aaron, will lead the Hebrews into the Promised Land.

argue that the people there are too well armed. Some Hebrews are fearful and want to return to Egypt.

Angry that the Hebrews are hesitating, God says he should wipe them out and start over. Moses pleads on their behalf and says it would dishonor God's name if his people were destroyed. To punish the Hebrews for their lack of faith, God

Biblical Mathematics

The number 40 occurs often in the Bible, typically referring to a period of testing spanning days, weeks, or years. Depending on the outcome of the trial, there is either a blessing or a punishment.

Genesis 7:17

TEST: The rain fell on the earth for 40 days and 40 nights, causing the Great Flood. **BLESSING:** God gave the rainbow as a sign that he would never destroy the world by water again.

Numbers 13:25

TEST: The 12 spies spent 40 days in Canaan assessing the land. **PUNISHMENT:** When 10 of the spies suggest it is dangerous to attack Canaan, the Hebrews rebel. God condemns them to wander the wilderness for 40 years until all the adult men are dead.

Deuteronomy 9:9

TEST: Moses spent 40 days without food or water while on Mt. Sinai. **BLESSING:** God rewarded Moses with the Ten Commandments.

Matthew 4:2

TEST: Jesus goes into the desert and fasts for 40 days. **BLESSING:** Although hungry, Jesus is able to withstand Satan's temptation to turn a stone into bread.

Acts 1:3

TEST: The time between Jesus's resurrection and ascension is 40 days. During this period, he appears to his disciples. **BLESSING:** Jesus's mission is completed and he ascends to Heaven.

VERSE TO KNOW

"I hereby command you:
Be strong and courageous;
do not be frightened or
dismayed, for the Lord your
God is with you wherever
you go." (Joshua 1:9)

ROCK OF AGES
Memorials of piled stones
were and still are an integral
part of the Jewish religion.

Today, some Jews still
place small stacks of stones
upon the graves of loved
ones, showing that they
have visited the grave and
remember the deceased.

JOSHUA 1

Joshua: The New Moses

THE HEBREWS GET A DIFFERENT LEADER.

God is clear about Joshua's role as the new Hebrew leader.

He instructs Joshua to "be strong and courageous" three different times in the opening verses and emphasizes the importance of obeying the laws given to the Hebrews through Moses. **(Joshua 1:2-9)**

Acting on God's admonition, Joshua sets in motion plans to invade Canaan. Joshua reminds the Hebrews that God promised them a land of their own, and warns that they will have to enter as armed warriors to claim Canaan. The Hebrews accept Joshua as their leader and urge him on with God's words:

"Be strong and courageous." **(Joshua 1:18)**

Joshua sends two spies to see what the Hebrews will face in Jericho. The spies enter through the house of a prostitute, Rahab, who pleads with the men to spare the lives of her family. She acknowledges that the

▲ *Joshua passing the River Jordan with the Ark of the Covenant*, by Benjamin West (ca. 1800)

citizens of Jericho are terrified of the Hebrews and promises to keep their location a secret in exchange for saving her loved ones.

RAHAB HELPS THE HEBREW SPIES

Word of the spies reaches the King of Jericho, who sends soldiers directly to Rahab's house to capture the intruders. When the king's men pound on Rehab's door, she hides the Hebrews and lies to the soldiers, saying the pair must have snuck out through the city gates.

Grateful, the spies tell Rehab that when the Hebrews attack, she must gather her family into her home and hang a crimson cord from her window so they know which house to spare.

Hearing about the events in Jericho, Joshua is ready to proceed. He commands the camp's priests to carry the Ark of the Covenant and to stop in the center of the Jordan River. When the priests wade into the river, the waters part, just as the Red Sea did for Moses, and the Hebrew army is able to cross safely.

Following orders from God, Joshua then selects one representative from each of the 12 tribes. He tells the men to place stones in the middle of the Jordan where the priests can rest the Ark temporarily.

Once this work is complete, the priests may carry the Ark to the far shore and let the waters rush back in. Joshua announces that in the future, people will see the stones and remember the miracle at the river.

▲ Robert Leinweber portrays Joshua and the Israelite army in *Destruction of the Walls of Jericho.* (1754)

Before the Hebrews enter the Promised Land, they must comply with a special covenant requiring the circumcision of all males born since the exodus from Egypt.

The ritual, outlined by Abraham in Genesis 17, is soon completed, and Joshua leads the people in the Passover feast, celebrating with food from their new land. This is the first day that the Hebrews don't have to rely on manna from heaven—a true sign that they have entered the land God promised to them. **(Joshua 5:12)**

TARGETING JERICHO

It is now time for the Hebrews to prepare for their first battle to capture Canaan. They have targeted the city of Jericho and will follow an unconventional plan of attack devised by God. Instead of ambushing the city with spears, arrows, rocks, or swords, the priests of Israel will simply walk around the walls of the city for seven days. On the seventh day, seven priests will sound their trumpets, and the walls of Jericho will collapse.

The Hebrews enter the city, killing all in their path except Rahab and those in her household. They burn the city of Jericho to the ground.

THE SUN STANDS STILL
After the destruction of Jericho, the reputation of the Hebrews spreads rapidly. They are approached by the city of Gibeon to make a peace treaty. Adoni-Zedek, the ruler of a rival kingdom, the Amorites of Jerusalem, forms an alliance with five powerful Amorite kings. This new alliance, called The Five Kings, makes plans to attack Gibeon.

The Gibeonites hear that the Five Kings are preparing to besiege their city. They quickly send word to Joshua. Joshua rallies his troops, and after an all-night march, he and his army launch a surprise assault on the Amorites. To give the Israelites more daylight to fight by, God stops the sun in the sky over Gibeon for a full day.

The battle ends, Gibeon is saved, and the armies of the Five Kings are defeated.

▲ Tel es-Sultan in Israel is the name of a long-term archaeology dig in the ancient city of Jericho.

VERSE TO KNOW
"Remove the sandals from your feet, for the place where you stand is holy."
(Joshua 5:15)

67

Samson in his final act as Judge in *Samson and Delilah and the Destruction of the Temple* by an unknown artist. (ca. 19th century)

CHAPTER 4

JUDGES FOR THE NATION

The death of Joshua leaves the Israelites leaderless in the land of Canaan. Instead of relying on a central government with a single ruler, the 12 tribes form a loose confederation. During this period of instability, a group of individuals known as the Judges emerge to guide the Hebrews.

The Cycle of Apostasy in Judges

Israel serves the Lord
↓
Israel falls into sin & idolatry
↓
Israel is enslaved
↓
Israel cries out to the Lord
↓
God raises up a Judge
↓
Israel is delivered

Samson Slays a Thousand Men by James Tissot (1901)

VERSE TO KNOW

"Then the Lord raised up judges, who delivered them out of the power of those who plundered them."
(Judges 2:16)

Rulers of Law

Kings and Judges both lead the people, but their powers and reigns are different.

Military Power
KING Commander in Chief
JUDGE Commands only during time of crisis

Governmental Authority
KING Head of State
JUDGE Rules only during time of crisis

Length of Rule
KING Lifetime appointment
JUDGE Serves temporarily, to deliver the people

Rules of Succession
KING Passes crown to offspring
JUDGE No hereditary rights

JUDGES, JOSHUA

Judges Rise to Power

A NEW TYPE OF LEADER ARRIVES TO ADVISE AND GUIDE THE ISRAELITES.

The books of Judges and Joshua are often studied together for their complementary theological and historical accounts of the Israelites taking over Canaan. The Book of Joshua presents the conquest as sudden and total, with God delivering on his promise to give his people a new land. Judges relates the theological version of the story, with the Hebrews failing repeatedly to live up to their covenant with God. In this book, the people defeat the Canaanites over many years, and only after betraying God, surviving oppressors he sends, repenting, and returning to their faith.

CYCLE OF WOE

This pattern, in which the Israelites abandon then return to their religion, is called the Cycle of Apostasy. Each time the people transgress, God punishes them with a trial and sends a Judge to deliver them. The people see their errors and repent. Then as soon as the Judge dies, the people sin again, and the cycle repeats.

The Book of Judges can be broken into four main sections:

1. Conquest
2. The Cycle of Apostasy:
   - Sin
   - Punishment from foreign oppression
   - Repentance
   - Deliverance through a Judge
3. The story of each Judge
4. The fate of two of Jacob's sons, Dan and Benjamin

Gideon talks to an angel in *The Miracle of Fleece of Gideon* by Nicolas Dipre. (1500)

James Tissot depicts Ehud meeting the king of Moab to deliver a secret message—a thrust from a double-edged sword—in *Eglon Slain by Ehud*. (1902)

JUDGES 3:9–11

Led Astray

GOD DISPATCHES JUDGES TO GUIDE
THE DISOBEDIENT ISRAELITES.

Although Joshua and the Israelites successfully conquer Canaan, they are repeatedly led astray by their subjects. In response, God sends a series of judges to deliver his people from spiritual crisis.

OTHNIEL, FIRST IN LINE

Othniel, the first Judge after Joshua dies, is summoned after the Israelites stray from God and are enslaved for eight years by the king of Aram-Naharaim in Mesopotamia. When the Israelites call out for help, Othniel arrives, defeats the king's army, and ushers in a 40-year period of peace and independence. Othniel is the only Judge connected with the Tribe of Judah.

EHUD AND THE DOUBLE-EDGED SWORD

Ehud is called as Judge when the Israelites again turn from God and are oppressed by the Moabite king Eglon. Ehud is sent to meet Eglon and prepares for the encounter by having a blacksmith craft a double-edged short-sword. Ehud is left-handed, so he conceals the weapon in his right boot where it is not expected. During the meeting, Ehud tells Eglon he needs to meet with him alone and Eglon dismisses his servants. Ehud announces, "I have a message from God for you," draws his sword, and stabs the king in his abdomen. The blow is so deep it eviscerates the

▲ *Othniel*, the warrior judge, by James Tissot (ca. 1880)

king and the sword disappears into the wound. Ehud leaves it there to make a hasty escape.

In the town of Seraiah in Ephraim, Ehud rallies the Israelite tribes by blowing the shofar, or ram's horn. The people congregate quickly and foil the Moabites by cutting off the fords of the Jordan River. The Hebrews then invade Moab itself and kill 10,000 Moabite soldiers.

After the death of Eglon, there is peace in the land for 80 years.

Leading the Israelites

MAJOR JUDGES
Othniel
Ehud
Deborah
Gideon
Jephthah
Samson

MINOR JUDGES
Shamgar
Tola
Jair
Ibzan
Elon
Abdon

SOUND OF THE SHOFAR
A shofar is a musical instrument made of a horn, traditionally that of a ram, used for Jewish religious purposes.

As with the modern bugle, there are no keys on a shofar to control pitch. Instead, a player coaxes sound from the instrument by varying the lip position.

Traditionally, the shofar was used to announce holidays and the Jubilee year. It was also used to signal the start of a war or to send a message.

The blast of a shofar emanating from the thick cloud on Mount Sinai made the Israelites tremble in awe. (Exodus 19:16)

Today, the shofar is typically blown on the Jewish holy days.

▲ *Jael Calling to Barak and His Men* by Arthur Dixon (ca. 1920)

DEBORAH, BRAVE AND WISE

Deborah is the only female Judge mentioned in the book. She is called to deliver the Israelites from Jabin, the king of Canaan, who has oppressed the people for 20 years.

God tells Deborah to prevail upon Barak, the captain of the Israelite army, to challenge the commander of Jabin's forces in battle. In spite of the fact that Jabin and his troops have superior weaponry, including 900 iron chariots, the Israelite force of 10,000 follows Deborah's advice and is triumphant.

In her discussions with Barak, Deborah prophesies that the honor of killing the other army's general will be given to a

Jael drives a tent peg through the skull of the Canaanite commander in *Jael and Sisera* by Bartolomeo Guidobono. (end of the 17th century)

woman. When Barak wins the battle, the losing general flees and seeks refuge in the tent of a young woman named Jael. With apparent goodwill, Jael "brought him curds in a lordly bowl." After the general drinks, he lies down and sleeps, and Jael drives a tent peg through his temple with such force that it enters the ground. Thus, Deborah's prophesy comes true. God allows a woman to kill the great general, the ultimate in humiliation for the Canaanites.

Deborah and Jael's victory is a turning point in the Israelites battles with Jabin, and as Israel grows stronger, it eventually defeats him. Then there is peace for 40 years.

APPROXIMATE TIMELINE OF THE JUDGES

Othniel	1350–1302 B.C.
Ehud	1302–1204 B.C.
Deborah	1204–1144 B.C.
Gideon	1191–1144 B.C.
Samson	1118–1078 B.C.

Gideon Surprising the Army of the Midianites by unknown artist (1754)

▲ Gideon chooses his 300 warriors after watching how they drink from the stream in *The Call of Gideon* by Arthur Dixon. (ca. 1920)

HUMBLE GIDEON

Gideon is a reluctant Judge, unsure of himself and of God's call to help the Israelites defeat their conquerors, the Midianites. Before he will accept his role, Gideon insists that God provide three signs. First, Gideon wants the angel of the Lord to cause a rock to burst into flames, consuming its meat and bread offering. Gideon then asks God to make his fleece rug wet with dew, while the ground is dry. Lastly, he requests the situation be reversed, so that the fleece is dry and the ground is wet. When God executes all these miracles, Gideon accepts his mission.

WHEN FEWER IS BETTER

To defeat the Midianites, God instructs Gideon to make their army turn on itself. Though Gideon has more than 22,000 men volunteer to help in this battle, God wants

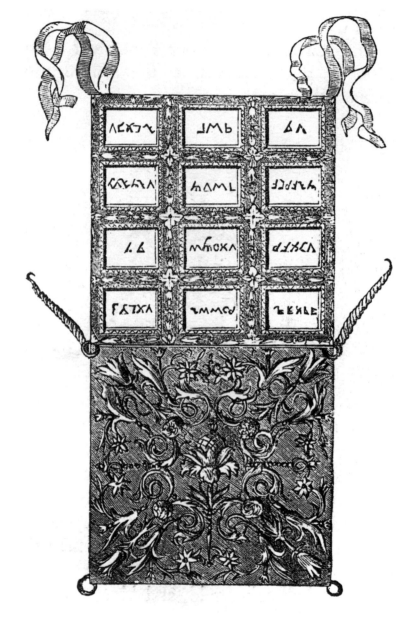

to win using only a fraction of those troops to reflect his divine power. Gideon narrows his forces to 300 men and provides each soldier with a shofar and a torch hidden in a clay pot. He instructs them to surround the enemy camp at night, and at a signal, to simultaneously break the pots, blow the horns, and blind the Midianites with torch light. The attack successfully disorients the enemy, which retreats.

The Israelites beg Gideon to be their king, but he refuses, asserting that only God is their ruler. He does, however, embrace his new power in subtle ways. He fashions an ephod, or a priestly breastplate, out of the gold won in battle. Gideon also names one of his 70-plus sons Abimelech, which means, "my father is king."

Peace prevails in Israel for 40 years, but as soon as Gideon dies of old age, the Israelites return to worshiping a false god.

▲ An illustration of an ephod or breastplate worn by the high priest (ca. 1700)

VERSE TO KNOW
"But I will be with you, and you shall strike down the Midianites, every one of them." (Judges 6:16)

The Sacrifice of Jephthah's Daughter by Giovanni Battista (ca. 1730)

JEPHTHAH'S HARD PATH

Jephthah is the illegitimate son of Gilead, a great-grandson of Joseph, and a prostitute. As Gilead's legitimate sons grow up, they fear Jephthah will inherit his father's wealth, and they force their half-brother to leave town. While subsisting on the outskirts of the village,

> "Jephthah feels he has no choice but to fulfill his vow and sacrifice his daughter."

Jephthah develops a band of followers who go on raids with him. This hard life makes Jephthah into a great warrior.

Soon, the Israelites are attacked by the Ammonites, and Jephthah's half-brothers go to him to convince him to be their general. Jephthah wants a more exalted position and agrees on the condition that if he wins the war, he will be the

leader of the Israelites for life.

At first, Jephthah tries to negotiate with the Ammonites using diplomacy, a tactic that fails. Then the spirit of the Lord comes upon Jephthah, and he makes God a promise. "If you will give the Ammonites into my hand, then whoever comes out of the doors of my house to meet me, when I return victorious from the Ammonites, shall be the Lord's, to be offered up by me as a burnt offering." **(Judges 11:30-31)**

The Daughter of Jephthah by an unknown artist (1643)

SACRIFICE BECOMES PERSONAL

Jephthah wins the battle but the bargain he struck with God turns bitter. When he returns home, the first person to come out of Jephthah's house is his only child, a daughter. Jephthah is filled with anguish, tears his clothes, and cries,

"Alas, my daughter! You have brought me very low; you have become the cause of great trouble to me!" **(Judges 11:35)**

Yet Jephthah feels he has no choice but to fulfill his vow and sacrifice his daughter.

Soon, the Ephraimites start attacking the Israelites for trespassing on their land while fighting with the Ammonites. Jephthah rallies and defeats the Ephraimites.

HOW DO YOU SAY "SHIBBOLETH"?

As Jephthah and his troops cross back over the River Jordan, they begin to encounter war refugees. Jephthah suspects that Ephraimites are masquerading as Israelites. He orders his men ask the refugees to say the word *Shibboleth*, knowing that the Ephraimites say *Sibboleth* with an *s* at the beginning of the word instead of *sh* as is the Hebrew custom. Once his soldiers hear the mispronounced word, they kill the offending Ephraimite. The Israelite army kills as many as 42,000 men this way.

Samson Threatens his Father-in-Law by Rembrandt (1635)

▲ Luca Giordano portrays Samson's courage in *Samson in the Lion's Den.* (17th century)

JUST SAY NO

According to the Book of Numbers, a Nazarite is a man or a woman who voluntarily promises to abstain from wine or intoxicating liquors, and from eating or drinking any substance that contains any trace of grapes. Nazarites also refrain from cutting their hair.

STRENGTH OF SAMSON

An angel comes to Manoah, a member of the tribe of Dan, and tells him that his wife is to refrain from alcohol because she is carrying a child that will be a Nazarite from birth and that the child will free the Israelites from the Philistines. When the baby is born, the couple names him Samson, and the mother promises he will never drink alcohol, shave, or cut his hair, as proof of his dedication to God. Thus, Samson is granted God's strength.

A WEAKNESS FOR WOMEN

Samson develops a weakness for Philistine women who betray him.

The first is a woman from Timnah. On his way to propose marriage to her, Samson is attacked by a lion. With God's strength, Samson is able to kill the lion with his bare hands, and the woman agrees to be his wife. Returning from their wedding, Samson notices that bees have made a nest in the carcass of the lion. As he eats some of the honey, he composes a riddle for the Philistine groomsmen who are attending him. He makes a bet: If the groomsmen can't answer the riddle, they will have to pay him 30 linen garments. But if they do answer, Samson will have to pay the 30 garments. The men agree, and he produces this riddle:

"Out of the eater came something to eat.

Out of the strong came something sweet."

The groomsmen can't come up with an answer and blame the bride and her family for humiliating them. They tell her that if she doesn't get the answer for them, they will burn her and her family to death. The woman coaxes the answer out of Samson.

▲ *Samson Kills a Thousand Philistines with the Jawbone of an Ass* by Gustave Doré (1832)

When the groomsmen recite the answer for Samson, he flies into a rage and kills them all. Returning home to see his wife, Samson finds out her father has given her to another man. This sends him into another killing rampage.

SLAYS 1,000 WITH THE JAWBONE OF AN ASS
In retaliation, the Philistines burn Samson's wife and father-in-law to death. Samson escalates the conflict by killing thousands of Philistines. He is hiding in a cave when he is finally cornered by the Philistines. To save the 3,000 men who are trying to protect him, Samson gives himself up. But when he is in the middle of the Philistine army, he breaks his shackles, picks up a jawbone of an ass, slays 1,000 Philistine soldiers, and escapes.

▲ Samson relaxes while Delilah prepares her scissors in *Samson and Delilah* by an unknown artist. (1609)

Samson soon meets Delilah, another Philistine woman, and falls in love again. Spies for the Philistines convince her to discover the secret to Samson's fierce powers. For many nights in a row Samson tells Delilah a different story, but finally he admits the truth, that his hair is the source of his strength. While her lover sleeps on her lap, Delilah allows the Philistines to cut his hair. For this, Samson is abandoned by God.

The Philistines poke out Samson's eyes and throw him in prison. He repents and regrows his hair, repairing his relationship with God. Preparing to publicly sacrifice Samson to their god, the Philistines bring him to the front of a temple. Crowds flock in to get a glimpse of the famous Samson and rejoice that he will die.

In his last act as a Judge of Israel, Samson uses the strength God gives him to pull down the pillars of the temple, killing many Philistines who have gathered round and all of their rulers.

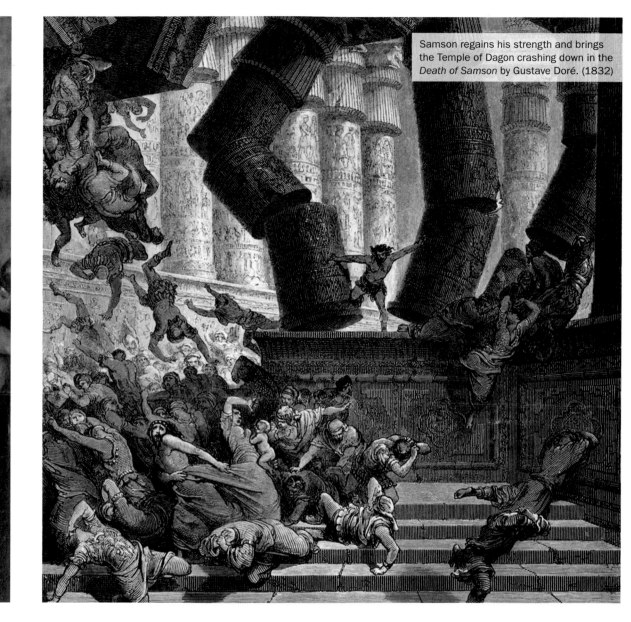

Samson regains his strength and brings the Temple of Dagon crashing down in the *Death of Samson* by Gustave Doré. (1832)

DOWNWARD CYCLE

Time and again in the Book of Judges the Israelites break their covenant with the Lord and embrace the Canaanite gods. They repeatedly suffer the consequences.

In contrast, God is faithful throughout the book and continually delivers his people from disaster. He is constant, not because Israel is deserving but because he is compassionate.

> "God is faithful . . . and continually delivers his people . . ."

The Judges though, are no angels. Even as they rescue the Israelites, they often contribute to the downward cycle. Major Judges such as Gideon, Jephthah, and Samson are guilty of significant sins, and only Deborah, the prophetess and warrior, proves to be the exception.

By the end of Judges, we see that Israel needs a king to lead in doing right in God's eyes rather than a leader who does "what was right in [his] own eyes." **(Judges 17:6)**

HERE COMES THE SUN?

Some scholars see the story of Samson as a variant of the myth of the Sun God.

- **Name:** Samson's name *Shimshon*, which means "man of the sun," is a variant of *Shamash*, the Babylonian Sun God. It is also the Hebrew name for the Sun.
- **Hair:** In the Sun God myth, the beams of light from the Sun God's head were mistaken for long, uncut hair.

1 SAMUEL 1:1–3:18
A Promised Child

A LATE-LIFE BABY RAISED BY A HIGH PRIEST
BECOMES THE LAST JUDGE OF ISRAEL.

Samuel, the last Judge and the first prophet, serves an important transitional role between the Judges and the kings.

The First Book of Samuel begins with a description of a woman, Hannah, who is barren and miserable. She goes to temple to pray to God for a child and is observed by Eli, a high priest. At first, Eli sees the woman's lips moving and thinks she is drunk. But upon hearing Hannah's words, he is moved by her sincere desire for a baby. When Hannah promises God that she will dedicate her child to him if she conceives, Eli blesses her. Hannah's prayers soon are answered and she names the baby Samuel. After he is weaned, she leaves the child in Eli's care.

Samuel is about 12 years old when he first hears God speaking to him. Initially he thinks the voice is Eli's, so he goes to the priest but is told to return to bed. After this happens three times, Eli realizes that God is speaking to Samuel. He instructs the boy to talk with God, who tells Samuel that Eli's sons are so wicked that Eli's dynasty will be condemned. Eli asks Samuel to honestly recount the conversation he has had with God. Though Eli has been aware of his sons' behavior, he knows he has not removed them from their priestly duties. Hearing the bad news, Eli acknowledges that God should do what is right.

HIGH PRIESTS
The priests of the Hebrew Scriptures are chosen to be spiritual leaders of the people. They are responsible for the sacred services, perform the sacrifices, maintain the Kosher Laws, and are the ones God speaks to directly when he has a message for the people.

VERSE TO KNOW
"Let your servant find favor in your sight." (I Samuel 1:18)

WHAT'S IN A NAME?
In Hebrew, *Samuel* means "God hears," "Asked of God," or "Name of God."

Hannah Presenting Her Son Samuel to the High Priest Eli by Lambert Doomer (ca. 1655)

▲ The Philistines return the Ark in *The Ark Sent Away* by James Tissot. (ca. 1900)

SAMUEL'S TURN

Once Eli dies, Samuel becomes a Judge. He uses his position to fight the Philistines, to keep the Israelites focused on God, and to settle local disputes among the people. But Samuel's sons, like Eli's, are corrupt, and the people are worried about submitting to their decisions. They demand that Israel be given a king.

Samuel opposes the appointment of a sovereign and gives a speech explaining his reasoning. Among other things, he says a king will require males to fight in his army and will levy heavy taxes on his citizens. But the Israelites insist, and Samuel reluctantly concedes.

He decides that the best way to choose the new ruler is to draw lots. Saul, the largest and strongest man in all of the tribes, is selected, and the people are temporarily satisfied.

When Saul loses God's favor, Samuel comes out of retirement and anoints the warrior David as the new king.

Eli questions Samuel regarding his vision, by an unknown artist (1900)

▲ *The Harvest of Ruth*, a miniature from a Latin Bible from Saint Amand's Abbey, France (16th century)

THE LOYALTY OF RUTH

In this book, Ruth, a widowed Moabite, finds God through her first husband and his family. Hers is a story of love, loyalty, and hardship.

The narrative starts with a famine in Israel. Seeking food, Elimelech, his wife Naomi, and their sons Mahlon and Chilion emigrate to the nearby country of Moab. In time, the sons marry two Moabite women: Mahlon takes Ruth as a wife and Chilion pairs with Orpah. Soon after, however, all three men die.

Heartbroken, Naomi decides to return to Israel and tells her daughters-in-law to rejoin their own mothers and find new husbands. Orpah reluctantly goes to her family; Ruth, however, refuses, declaring to Naomi, "Your people are my people, your God is my God."

Summer (Ruth and Boaz) from Seasons by Nicolas Poussin (ca. 1640)

Ruth and Naomi travel to Bethlehem, where it is the beginning of the barley harvest. Through her husband's family, Naomi has a wealthy kinsman named Boaz with a barley field. Since the two women have little to eat, Naomi asks Boaz if Ruth may trail his harvest workers and pick up kernels they leave behind, a practice known as gleaning. Boaz agrees and is kind to Ruth because he has heard about her loyalty to her mother-in-law. He tells Ruth he has asked the other workers to help her and that she should be rewarded for her deeds.

As a close relative of the family of Naomi's husband, Boaz is obliged by law to marry Ruth in order to carry on his family's inheritance. Eventually, Boaz and Ruth are married and produce a son named Obed, who is "the father of Jesse, the father of David."

REDEEMER KINSMAN
When an Israelite man dies without leaving a male offspring, his brother is supposed to take the widow as his wife and produce a child with her so that the deceased brother's name will live on.

Naomi sends Ruth to Boaz to invoke him to "redeem" her by marrying her—which is what happens.

CHAPTER 5

THE NATION WANTS A KING

The Israelites reject God as their ruler and demand that Samuel give them a human leader.

Giovanni Lanfranco depicts David's victory over Goliath in *The Triumph of David*. (1605)

1 SAMUEL 8-11, 13

Saul, the First King

THE PEOPLE DEMAND A RULER FOR
PROTECTION FROM OTHER NATIONS.

Scholars do not know how old Saul is when he becomes king of Israel, nor how long he reigns. The best Hebrew manuscripts don't list these figures. The text is clear, however, that the rule of Israel's first king was troubled from the beginning.

The narrative begins with the Israelites asking God for a human king who can protect them from other nations. God tasks the prophet Samuel with a search, but Samuel protests and tells the Hebrews that God too is opposed to the idea. In time, God overrides Samuel's objections and instructs him to select a strong warrior.

Saul's reign starts well when he defeats an Ammonite king who attacks the Israelite town of Jabesh. But preparing for another battle, Saul alienates Samuel by performing ritual sacrifices reserved for prophets. When Samuel arrives at the end of the ceremony, he tells Saul he will be replaced by someone who will do his duty and obey God. Over time, Saul listens less and less to God and Samuel.

The relationship between Samuel and Saul is finally severed when Saul disobeys God's instructions to wipe out the Amalekites and their cattle: he instead takes the Amalekite king as a personal trophy and allows his men to keep the cattle as their prize. Samuel withdraws his support of Saul and never sees the king again.

It is the beginning of the end for Saul.

ANOINTING

Among the Hebrews, anointing oil is a significant part of consecration and is used to confer holiness on the object or person being anointed. Initially, only high priests and sacred vessels were anointed. But kings and prophets were later included in the sacrament.

Sometimes, the high priest and king were referred to as "the anointed." In Israel, a king needed to be anointed by a prophet but did not need a crown.

Saul Prophesies With the Prophets by James Tissot (1902)

▲ *Samuel Anointing Saul* by an unknown artist (1754)

Dutch artist Abraham Bloemaert's engraving shows Saul cut down in battle in *Death of Saul*. (16th century)

The young warrior is in a pensive mood in *David Contemplating the Head of Goliath* by Orazio Gentileschi. (1612)

1 SAMUEL 16-2 SAMUEL 1
Samuel Anoints Saul's Successor

DAVID ARISES FROM OBSCURITY TO
BECOME THE SECOND KING OF ISRAEL.

David is one of the most well known of all the biblical heroes. He is the youngest, smallest son of a shepherd; he famously kills a giant while still a boy; he is a gifted musician and writer; he is a handsome lady's man; he is a cunning general; and no matter how badly he behaves, he never seems to lose God's favor. During David's 40-year rule, he unites the people of Israel into a strong nation, conquers new lands, and paves the way for his son, Solomon, to build the Temple.

David begins his ascent to power while Saul is still king. Without Saul's knowledge, God sends a successor, and Samuel travels to visit the family of Jesse of Bethlehem, the grandson of Ruth the Moabite. Jesse parades his seven grown sons in front of Samuel, but Samuel asks to see the youngest son, David, who is out with the sheep. Samuel then blesses the family and anoints David, who returns to his flock. It is said that the "Spirit of the Lord came mightily upon David" and at the same time deserted Saul.

David's first interaction with Saul comes when the king is looking for someone to play music to ease his headaches and bad temper and an attendant summons David. The boy's playing pleases Saul and he keeps David close.

> **VERSE TO KNOW**
> "Do not look on his appearance or on the height of his stature, because I have rejected him; for the Lord does not see as mortals see; they look on the outward appearance, but the Lord looks on the heart." (**1 Samuel 16:7**)

Felix-Joseph Barrias shows the young David being chosen by God in *Anointing of David by Samuel*. (1842)

SHADOW IMAGE
Some believers think that some characters in the Old Testament foreshadowed the life of Christ.
Isaac: 1) Isaac carries the wood for the sacrifice on his back; Jesus carries a wooden cross. 2) Abraham (father) is willing to sacrifice his son; God, Jesus's father, does sacrifice his son. 3) Before Abraham sacrifices Isaac, a lamb is found; Jesus is called the Lamb of God. (**John 1:29**)
David: 1) Both were born in Bethlehem; 2) David was a shepherd; Christ, the Good Shepherd; 3) The five stones chosen to slay Goliath are parallel to the five wounds of Christ; 4) David is betrayed by his trusted counselor, Achitophel; Jesus is betrayed by Judas.

STRINGS ATTACHED
King David mastered a number of stringed instruments including the lyre, but one of the most interesting and least familiar is the ancient kinnor.

Featuring a rectangular or trapezoidal sound box, the kinnor has two curved arms of unequal length that are joined by a crossbar. Typically, a musician strums the kinnor's 10 strings with his or her fingers.

Thanks to a light framework and high-tension strings, the kinnor is loud enough to compete with rams' horns, trumpets, and cymbals.

I SAMUEL 17
David and Goliath

A BOY DEFEATS A GIANT IN AN EPIC BATTLE.

The first time David publicly displays his courage is when, as an inexperienced boy armed with only a stick and a few stones, he confronts an armored Philistine giant, Goliath of Gath.

At this time, it is common for an army to send out a warrior to battle a member of the opposing force. Both factions agree that the winner will claim victory for his side.

David volunteers to face Goliath after skilled warriors cower in fear for 40 days. Saul, the king, tries to suit David up in armor and weapons, but none are small enough to fit him. Wearing only his daily clothes, David makes a slingshot, invokes God's name, and kills the giant with his first shot. He then chops off Goliath's head, prompting the Philistines to flee in terror.

Impressed, Saul takes David on as commander of his troops, but he soon grows jealous of David's successes and tries many times to kill him.

David forms a close friendship with Saul's son, Jonathan. Later, when Saul tries to enlist Jonathan in a plot to kill David, it is Jonathan who warns David to escape.

Italian painter Tiziano Vecelli, known in English as Titian, portrays David giving thanks after his victory in *David and Goliath*. (ca. 1544)

3,50		3,50
3,00		3,00
2,50		2,50
2,00		2,00
1,50		1,50
1,00		1,00
0,50		0,50
0		0
GOLITH 1,97m	ANCIENT MAN 1,60 m	TELGEZER 1,955 m

A GROWING LEGEND

With successive retelling of the David and Goliath tale, the giant has grown taller.

The oldest manuscripts, including the Dead Sea Scrolls, the 1st-century historian Josephus, and the 4th-century Septuagint, all give Goliath's height as "four cubits and a span" (6 feet 9 inches).

In later tellings, the giant's height is "six cubits and a span" (9 feet 9 inches).

WHO ARE YOU CALLING A PHILISTINE?

The Philistines appear in the southern coastal area of Canaan at the beginning of the Iron Age (ca. 1175 B.C.). They are often referred to as Sea People.

It's assumed that the Philistines are Indo European speakers from around the coast of Asia Minor.

Recent discoveries indicate that the Sea People, sometimes portrayed as backwards, were not as uneducated and uncultured as the Israelites made them out to be.

▲ Fueled by jealousy, Saul attempts to murder David, portrayed here in *Saul Versus David* by Giovanni Francesco Barbieri. (1646)

VERSE TO KNOW
"For everything there is a season, and a time for every matter under heaven." (Ecclesiastes 3:1)

WHAT A DIFFERENCE A KING MAKES
Before the Israelites have a king, their arms are primitive, made of stone and wood. They rely heavily on surprise raids to protect their mountain lands.

Once Saul is anointed king, he passes on his warrior skills to his troops. He trains the Israelite army to use iron weapons, and his soldiers soon are able to eject nomads from the plains and capture cities.

2 SAMUEL
A Military Leader Is Born

SAUL PLOTS A MURDER.

Saul watches jealously as David triumphs on and off the battlefield and vows to kill him. He tries many times but fails and finally declares a truce. Saul shows his good will by giving David his daughter Michal in marriage—but his hatred continues to seethe, and David ultimately is forced to flee Israel.

Finding refuge with the king of Moab, David begins a campaign to win support for his own army. He and his band of men raid nomadic tribes and hand the spoils to the leaders of Judah. During this time, Saul and his son Jonathan are killed on Mt. Gilboa. David mourns deeply for both of them and moves his household to the city of Hebron in Judah. The citizens are grateful to the warrior for saving them from the nomads and appoint David king of Judah.

As leader, David helps Judah become stronger than Israel. He is approached by Saul's son Abner who proposes an end to the rivalry between the kingdoms. David agrees, but then, without his permission, a rogue army commander kills Abner. Soon, another of Saul's sons, Ishbaal, is also murdered, and David moves to unite Judah and Israel. The prophet Samuel, with blessings of all the tribes of Israel, anoints David as their king.

David's first action is to capture Jerusalem, which became the City of David, to fortify it, and to build himself a palace. He moves the Ark to Jerusalem and plans to erect a permanent temple where the Israelites may worship in safety. But God tells the new king that building it will be the job of David's son.

David attacks the Ammonites in Gustave Doré's *Siege of Rabbah*. (ca. 1870)

King David Bearing the Ark of the Covenant into Jerusalem by an unknown artist (1753)

▲ David is enraptured by the beautiful Bathsheba in Jan Massys' *David and Bathsheba* (1562)

2 SAMUEL 11-12

Falling for Bathsheba

DAVID ABUSES HIS POWER AND TAKES THE WIFE OF ONE OF HIS GENERALS.

BRAVE NEW WORLD

In the time of Judges, a prophet's job was to serve as spokesman for God and as a leader. But when Nathan takes Samuel's place as prophet, he has an additional responsibility: standing up to the king. This role is fraught with many dangers, but Nathan has the courage to confront David, to tell him to repent for his sins and to urge him to change his ways.

David shows great cunning and wisdom in leading his nation, but he is reckless in his personal life. One day while his men are away at war, David spies a beautiful woman, Bathsheba, from his rooftop. He inquires about her and learns she is the wife of one of his generals. David sends for Bathsheba who conceives a child. At first David tries to fool the general, Uriah, into believing he is the father. He summons Uriah from war and suggests

he return home. But Uriah refuses to lay with his wife while his men are still in battle. David arranges for Uriah to be killed during a dangerous mission so that he can marry Bathsheba.

Nathan the prophet confronts David, who admits his sin. As punishment, Bathsheba's child dies and David is cursed with the promise of a rebellion from within his own house. Bathsheba and David soon conceive a second son, Solomon.

Nathan the prophet rebukes David over his affair with Bathsheba in *David and the Prophet Nathan*, by Lorenzo Sabbatini. (16th century)

In *Tamar Crying on the Lap of Absalom*, French painter Alexandre Cabanel portrays Tamar's grief and Absalom's rage following her rape by her half-brother Amnon. (1893)

2 SAMUEL
A Family in Trouble

DAVID'S SON ABSALOM REBELS AGAINST HIS AGING FATHER.

King David's family dynamics are the same as those of many rich, political families today. Greed, lust, and betrayal coexist with loyalty, forgiveness, and family bonds. David's personal situation worsens when his daughter, Tamar, is raped by her half-brother, Amnon. Absalom, who is David's son and Tamar's brother, retaliates, killing Amnon.

Absalom escapes, but after much soul searching David allows Absalom to return to Jerusalem.

OH, ABSALOM, ABSALOM!
Absalom is handsome, popular with the people of Israel, and ambitious. Convinced his father is weakening after 40 years as king, Absalom plots a rebellion. David and his followers flee

Jerusalem, leaving behind only 10 concubines, some priests, and a spy. Absalom reaches Jerusalem, takes over the city, and sleeps with David's concubines. The spy befriends Absalom and then sends messages to David through the priests. David gathers his troops and kills 20,000 of Absalom's Israelite soldiers and Absalom himself.

Italian Baroque artist Mattia Preti depicts the murder of Amnon in *The Banquet of Absalom.* (1660)

Absalom Says Goodbye to His Father King David by an unknown artist

David is said to have written Psalm 63 when he was hiding at the spring at Ein Gedi, pictured here.

▲ This book of Psalms from the 17th century sold for millions at a public auction.

FAMOUS PSALMS

David is credited with writing 73 of the 150 psalms. Here are some highlights:

Psalm 3:3-4

"But you, O Lord, are a shield around me,
    my glory, and the one who lifts up my head.
I cry aloud to the Lord,
    and he answers me from his holy hill."

Psalm 23:1-3

"The Lord is my shepherd, I shall not want.
He makes me lie down in green pastures;
    he leads me beside still waters;
    he restores my soul.
He leads me in right paths for his name's sake."

Psalm 51:10-12

"Create in me a clean heart, O God,
    and put a new and right spirit within me.
Do not cast me away from your presence,
    and do not take your holy spirit from me.
Restore to me the joy of your salvation,
    and sustain in me a willing spirit."

2 SAMUEL 22, PSALMS
David, the Writer of Psalms

MOST OF THE INDIVIDUAL VERSES IMAGINE A WORLD WHERE EVERYONE PRAISES GOD.

David, along with being an able ruler, has a way with music and words. He is believed by some to have written close to half of the 150 sacred hymns that make up the Book of Psalms, and many of the book's prayers are entitled "A Psalm of David." One of the Dead Sea Scrolls attributes 3,600 songs of praise to this talented king.

The words of the hymns express David's everyday thoughts, struggles, and prayers. They describe scenes in which David is forced to flee his enemies, in which he needs strength and help, gives thanks for victories, asks for vindication, prays when enemies defeat him, and prays for comfort.

Over the centuries, David's authorship has been called into question, with some biblical scholars suggesting that the ancients credited David as a way to link the psalms to Divine Inspiration. Today it is widely believed the psalms were written over five centuries, from the early Canaanite period to the end of exile. The majority of the hymns originate in the kingdom of Judah, where they were sung during Temple worship.

David plays the harp for his wife Micah in this painting by Virginio Grana called *David and Micol*. (19th century)

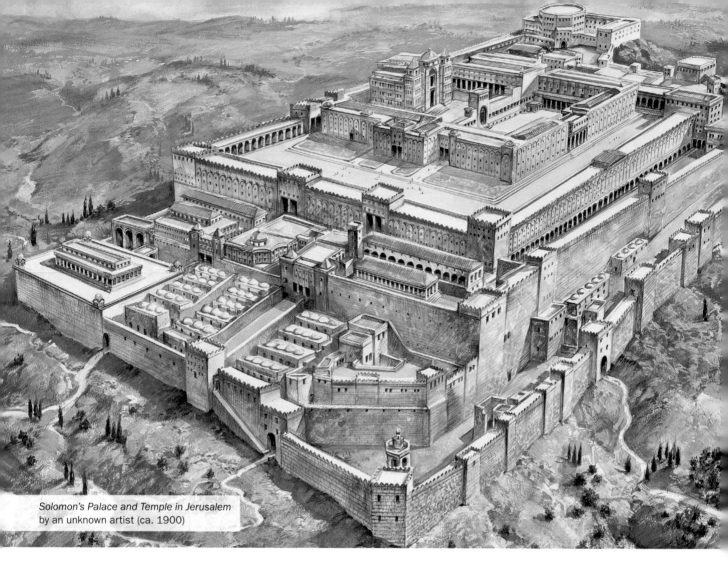

Solomon's Palace and Temple in Jerusalem by an unknown artist (ca. 1900)

THE TEMPLE
Solomon built the First Temple around 957 B.C. to replace the Tabernacle that Moses constructed in the Sinai Desert.

ECCLESIASTES
Although traditionally assigned to Solomon, scholars now think Ecclesiastes was written anonymously. One of the Wisdom Books of the Old Testament, the book explores the meaning of life and the best way one ought to live. Since both rich and poor alike die, the writer says, life has no clear meaning.

1 KINGS 5-9

Solomon, the Master Builder

THE KING CONSTRUCTS THE FIRST TEMPLE, A PALACE, AND MANY CITIES.

Once Solomon's empire is tranquil, he begins to erect the Temple, based on the plans that God gave King David. Solomon imposes compulsory labor service on both the Israelites and on the foreign nations under his control, and for seven years, the workers toil. When they are done, the edifice is unlike any other: It is made of stone and cedar, full of carvings, and overlaid with pure gold. To celebrate the Temple's completion, Solomon arranges a public dedication ceremony of prayers and sacrifices.

Solomon also uses slave labor from the Hittites, Amorites, Perizzites, Hivites, and Jebusites on a multitude of other construction projects. He spends 13 years creating his own palace and also puts up a wall around Jerusalem, a citadel called the Millo, a palace for a favored wife, and facilities for foreign traders. He erects cities for chariots and horsemen and creates

storage cities. He extends Jerusalem to the north and fortifies cities near the mountains.

SOLOMON AND HIS WIVES

Solomon further solidifies his rule through marital alliances, trade relationships, and colonization. It is said that he has 700 wives and 300 concubines. He has a large share in the trade between northern and southern countries. He establishes Israelite colonies around his province to look after military, administrative, and commercial matters. He divides his empire into 12 districts, with Judah constituting its own political unit and enjoying certain privileges.

A myriad of forces contribute to Solomon's downfall in his old age.

He allows his numerous foreign wives to worship other gods and make sacrifices; Solomon even builds an altar for them. He places heavy taxes on the people, who become bitter. He forces his people to work as soldiers, chief officers, and commanders. The special privileges granted the tribes of Judah begin to alienate the northern tribes. Finally, the prophet Ahijah of Shiloh declares that Jeroboam, son of Nebat, is to become king over 10 of the 12 tribes—not one of Solomon's sons.

After 40 years ruling Israel, Solomon dies and is buried in Jerusalem. His son Rehoboam takes over the remains of Solomon's empire. Under Rehoboam, the kingdom crumbles and finally is divided in two.

▲ *Solomon in the Temple Treasury* by Flemish painter Frans Francken II (1633)

▲ *The Cup of Solomon*, made of gold, rock crystal, garnet, and green glass bearing a relief cameo of a king, from the Sassanian Period (ca. 590–651 A.D.)

Job and His Children by Domenico Piola (ca. 1650)

▲ *The Destruction of Leviathan* by Gustave Doré (1865)

JOB
God Tests a Good Man

JOB SUFFERS, ARGUES WITH HIS FRIENDS, AND IS FINALLY RESTORED.

In the prose prologue to the story, Job is a prosperous and righteous man living in the land of Uz with his large family and flocks. One day, God points out to Satan that Job is a pious man. Satan responds that Job is good only because his life is going so well; if bad things were to begin to happen to him, Job would curse God. Disagreeing, God gives Satan permission to test Job's devotion as he wishes, short of taking his life.

Satan unleashes unthinkable punishments. He first kills Job's children and destroys his wealth. A bit later, he attacks Job physically, riddling his body with horrible boils. Even Job's wife turns on him, urging Job to "Curse God, and die," but Job refuses to do so. **(Job 2:9)**

Destitute and alone, Job is approached by three friends who attempt to comfort him.

From this point forward, the story is told in the form of poetic dialogs between Job

VERSE TO KNOW
"Naked I came from my mother's womb, and naked shall I return there; the Lord gave, and the Lord has taken away; blessed be the name of the Lord." **(Job 1:21)**

and his friends and between Job and God. Job, as the protagonist, is praised for his steadfast defense of his own righteousness and God's justice. He tries hard to find a way to justify God's actions. Job's friends argue that he must have done something to incur the wrath of God. How, they argue, would God allow such a good man to suffer? Today we might phrase this question as, "Why does God allow bad things to happen to good people?"

Though Job and his friends argue endlessly, there is no single victor. All make significant points and counterpoints using irony, sarcasm, and direct refutation.

As a storm gathers, God reveals himself to Job, and asks: *"Who is this that darkens counsel by words without knowledge?"* (**Job 38:2**) God then considers a list of mysteries so sublime and majestic he thinks Job and his friends

cannot possibly understand them. The list includes the following:

- How land and water are balanced so perfectly on Earth
- How the horse gets its strength
- How the constellations such as Orion, the Pleiades, Arcturus, and the signs of the Zodiac are set in the night sky
- How animals have different gestation periods but all reproduce and grow
- How the Leviathan is so huge and ferocious

Job has no answer for God and in the end, is satisfied that his Lord is just.

One conclusion to be drawn from these exchanges is that Job and his friends, because of their limited understanding and perspective, are unable to grasp the ineffable.

In the end, God restores to Job his former wealth. Job and his wife have more children.

▲ *The Book Of Job* from the Monastery of St. Catherine, Sinai, Egypt (ca. 11th century)

___

WHAT IS A LEVIATHAN?
The leviathan mentioned in Job Chapter 41 is a sea monster, a mythical beast of unimaginable strength and viciousness.

In modern literature such as *Moby Dick*, it refers to a whale.

Power passes from father to son in *King David Presenting the Sceptre to Solomon* by Cornelis de Vos. (ca. 17th century)

CHAPTER 6

THE NATION IS DIVIDED

The unity of the new nation of Israel is tenuous, held together largely by the personalities of its first three rulers. Solomon, the last of these monarchs, builds and expands the kingdom, but after his death, it splits in two.

▲ *The Prophet Jeremiah Mourning over the Destruction of Jerusalem* by Rembrandt (1630)

1 & 2 KINGS, 2 CHRONICLES
One God, Two Kingdoms

UNDER REHOBOAM, THE KINGDOM BREAKS APART.

With the rise of Rehoboam, Solomon's son, the stage is set for civil discord.

1 Kings, 2 Kings, and 2 Chronicles cover the collapse of

VERSE TO KNOW

"For surely I know the plans I have for you, says the Lord, plans for your welfare and not for harm, to give you a future with hope."
(Jeremiah 29:11)

the united kingdom of Israel but do so from two different perspectives. The Kings' accounts relate the history of both northern and southern territories, while 2 Chronicles deals only with the southern kingdom of Judah.

Tradition says the prophet Jeremiah, who witnessed the Babylonian exile, wrote 1 and 2 Kings. The Kings' narrative offers insight into how a nation declined and abandoned its religion.

Traditional authorship of Chronicles goes to Ezra,

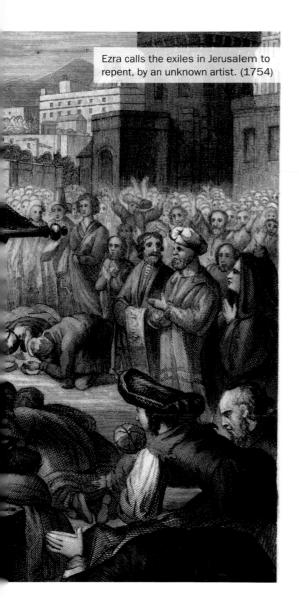

Ezra calls the exiles in Jerusalem to repent, by an unknown artist. (1754)

Mediterranean Sea

Asher

Naphtali

Sea of Galilee

Zebulun

Issachar

ISRAEL

Manasseh

Dan

Ephraim

Gad

Benjamin

Reuben

JUDAH

Dead Sea

Simeon

■ The Kingdoms of Israel
■ The Kingdoms of Judah

a scribe who lived during the restoration of Judah from its captivity. Ezra wrote Chronicles as a cautionary tale, to ensure that the people did not repeat their mistakes.

While Judah (in the south) and Israel (to the north) squabble with each other, the downfall of both nations comes at the hands of ancient empires.

During the height of its power, Assyria forces Israel into exile, while Judah is sent to Babylon roughly 130 years later.

During this period of social and political turmoil, prophets try to convince the people to reform their ways. Some write lengthy books of the finest poetry while others never write anything, leading a rough-hewn existence in the wilderness.

Covering a period of more than 300 years, the divided kingdom provides a body of literary work unique in genre, vast in scope, and deeply spiritual in tone.

> "During the height of its power, Assyria forces Israel into exile, while Judah is sent to Babylon roughly 130 years later."

▲ This map shows the division of Israel into 10 tribes in the northern kingdom, and two tribes of the southern kingdom of Judah.

The Division of the Kingdoms Under Rehoboam by William Hole (ca. 1899)

The Counsellors of Rehoboam Outside of Jerusalem by an unknown artist

1 KINGS 12; 2 CHRONICLES 10

A Harsh Leader Drives His People Away

REHOBOAM LOSES CONTROL.

After Rehoboam ascends the throne, the people send an envoy under the leadership of Jeroboam, an exiled revolutionary, to ask for tax relief. The older counselors advise Rehoboam to lighten the load, to speak diplomatically, and to make himself a servant of the people. The younger counselors advise him to discipline and treat his subjects harshly, which is what the new king does.

The strict treatment drives all the northern tribes to secede from the kingdom, leaving Rehoboam with nothing but his own tribe of Judah. The northern alliance of tribes, called Israel, rallies around Jeroboam. His dynasty is brief, however.

When Jeroboam's son becomes deathly ill, he sends his wife in disguise to Ahijah, the prophet in Judah in the south, to find out what will happen to the child.

But Ahijah sees through the disguise and predicts a violent death for Jeroboam's household because of his idolatry. The prophet says the only exception will be the sick child, who will die peacefully when the wife returns to Jeroboam and sets foot into their home.

After the death of Jeroboam, a series of short-lived kings follow one another in quick, bloody succession. Nadab, Baasha, Elah, and Zimri rise to power through violence and fall the same way. Omri, the captain of the army, succeeds Zimri, becomes king, and moves the capital to Samaria, where it remains for the rest of the kingdom.

GOLDEN CALVES, AGAIN?
Jeroboam, recognizing that traditional worship at the temple in Jerusalem will maintain ties to the south, sets up two rival religious sites with golden idols in the form of calves. He also promotes calf worship by offering sacrifices to them himself. This, according to **1 Kings 13:34**, ". . . became sin to the house of Jeroboam, so as to cut it off and to destroy it from the face of the earth." The act serves as a mark of apostasy for every subsequent northern king, because none of them ever remove the golden idols.

▲ In *Jezebel Advises Ahab*, James Tissot shows the influence Jezebel has on her husband. (ca. 1880)

AHAB—THE MOST EVIL KING IN ISRAEL

Succeeding Omri is Ahab, described as the most evil king in Israel's history. Ahab goes beyond Jeroboam's sin of building the golden calves by marrying Jezebel, a princess who encourages him to import Baal worship, and by taking a neighbor's land after conspiring to have him executed.

Offended by Ahab's behavior, God and the prophet Elijah seek to punish him. The episode starts when Elijah appears before the king and says, "As the Lord the God of Israel lives, before whom I stand, there shall be neither dew nor rain these years, except by my word." **(1 Kings 17:1)** Elijah then departs, leaving no word as to his whereabouts.

Elijah's prophecy to Ahab comes true; it

Prophets of Baal Sacrifice, from a Belgian tapestry showing Elijah's sacrifice burning on the altar (ca. 1150–1560)

WHO IS BAAL?
A better question is "Who are the Baals?" The Hebrew Bible sometimes refers to them in the plural (**Judges 8:33**), but the term is generally regarded as an honorific meaning "Lord" or "Master." Some scholars believe that Elijah was confronting priests of the Phoenician god of thunder, Melqart, as a rebuke to Jezebel, who was a Phoenician. This would explain why Elijah would use drought and rain to demonstrate the Lord's power.

stops raining. Three years into the drought, Elijah tells Ahab that he wants to arrange a battle between the God of Israel and Baal. Each side will build an altar and ask their god to send fire to burn the altar. The god who sends fire from heaven will be declared the true deity.

The followers of Baal build their altar and appeal all day to their god with no result.

Elijah then soaks his altar with water and offers a simple prayer. His point is made when fire burns the water-soaked structure.

Elijah slaughters the prophets of Baal and tells the king to hurry to his palace before he gets caught in the storm.

The book of 1 Kings closes when Ahab is mortally wounded by an arrow in a battle, and the army deserts the field.

▲ *War Between Asa and Baasha* by an unknown artist

1 KINGS 13–2 KINGS 8

Early Southern Rulers

A SERIES OF SPIRITUAL REFORMS HELPS
KEEP THE SOUTHERN KINGDOM TOGETHER.

The southern kingdom of Judah maintains a single dynastic reign throughout its history, reflecting God's promise to David that he would ". . . establish the throne of his kingdom forever." **(2 Samuel 7:13)** There are times when the

dynasty comes perilously close to ending, but the promise prevails.

Rehoboam permits the proliferation of idolatry, household shrines, and temple prostitutes.

This angers God, and Rehoboam

Barlaam and Jehoshaphat, a relief by Benedetto Antelami (ca. 12th century)

▲ The tomb of Jehoshaphat, on the right, in the Kidron Valley, Israel

is defeated by Egyptians, who sack the temple. The next king is Asa, who introduces religious reforms such as deposing the queen mother, eradicating institutional idol worship, and banishing the male prostitutes. Asa is generally regarded as a good ruler, although his alliance with the Aramaen king against Baasha of Israel signals the low point of his reign.

Jehoshaphat succeeds Asa and institutes

> "Asa is generally regarded as a good ruler, although his alliance . . . against Baasha . . . signals the low point of his reign."

even deeper spiritual reforms despite an ill-advised marital alliance between his son and Ahab's daughter.

When Jehoram ascends the throne in Israel, he implements a brutal purge, killing all his brothers and half-brothers to eliminate any threat to his reign. Jehoram is such a wicked king that Elijah, primarily a prophet of the north, sends him a letter cursing him for being so evil. Jehoram contracts a debilitating bowel disease and dies.

▲ *Athaliah Chased from the Temple* by Charles-Antoine Coypel (ca. 1725)

PURGES IN THE NORTH

The next king is Jehu, who purges all vestiges of Ahab in the northern territory of Israel. He even kills Ahab's grandson, Ahaziah, the heir to the Judean throne.

Athaliah, the mother of Ahaziah, is so enraged at the murder of her last surviving son that she goes on a bloody rampage. She kills all potential royal heirs she can find, hoping to forestall any conflict over the succession and then promptly places herself on the throne.

One heir who escapes Athaliah's slaughter is Joash, the infant son of Ahaziah. Joash and his nurse are rescued by the priest Jehoiada and hidden while Athaliah rules Judah for six years. Eventually Jehoiada assembles a revolutionary council to depose Athaliah and establish Joash as the rightful king.

The queen rushes to the temple to accuse Jehoiada of treason, but he orders guards to seize her and to put her to death outside the temple grounds.

Under the regency of Jehoiada, Joash embarks on a series of religious reforms, restoring temple worship to its formerly prominent place. However, the reforms only last as long as Jehoiada lives, because after his death, Joash lapses back into apostasy.

The Coronation of Joash and Death of Athaliah by William Hole (ca. 1880)

FOLLOW WHICH LEADER?

In ancient Palestine, most kings employ prophets as advisers. Politics and religion are so deeply intertwined that it is impossible, when reading the Bible, to separate them. This potent mix makes for an unexpected governmental structure.

- **Kings:** The king is the executive leader. His primary job is to lead his army in war. The king also adjudicates various high-level disputes that cannot be resolved by town and tribal elders, usually of a civic rather than religious nature.

- **Priests:** The descendants of Levi form a complex hierarchy of religious roles and functions, some executive and some judicial. Strictly speaking, the descendants of Aaron who perform ceremonial religious duties centered on the temple are considered priests. However, the rest of the descendants of Levi live in cities scattered throughout the land and serve in a support capacity. Priests interpret the law and settle disputes.

- **Prophets:** Prophets come to their role through a direct call from the Lord. Prophets serve as a check to balance any excesses of the king or apostate priestly class.

◀ *Elijah and the Angel* by Antonio Cavallucci (18th century)

The outline of the story is simple. God tells Jonah to go to Nineveh and tell the people there that if they don't repent, God is going to judge them.

Jonah refuses to go on grounds that Nineveh is both wicked and the capital of the Assyrian empire, foe to the Israelites. Instead, Jonah heads in the opposite direction, to a port town, and boards a ship going away from Ninevah.

Angry, God sends a violent storm that threatens to break up the ship. The sailors draw lots to determine who brought them the bad luck and discover it is Jonah. They throw him overboard, where he is swallowed by a large fish sent by God. From the belly of the fish, Jonah repents, cries out to God, and is saved.

After three days, the fish deposits Jonah on the shore. He goes to Nineveh and preaches repentance. To his utter surprise, the Ninevites heed his message and repent. God hears their repentance and does not destroy them.

Jonah, however, is bothered that the Ninevites are not judged. He complains to God, who tells Jonah that he should be concerned about the 120,000 people of Nineveh.

VERSE TO KNOW
"Deliverance belongs to the Lord!" (Jonah 2:9)

Many people miss the deeper meaning of the story of Jonah when they get stuck on the plausibility of a big fish swallowing a human—and his living inside of it for three days. The bigger story is that Jonah follows the Lord's call to preach judgment to a nation that will eventually destroy his own country. An even bigger miracle is that the Assyrians heed the message.

WHAT MAKES A PROPHET MAJOR OR MINOR?

Major Prophets are distinguished from the Minor Prophets not by importance, but by the size of the books they write. Accordingly, Isaiah, Jeremiah, and Ezekiel are considered Major Prophets. Interestingly enough, Elijah, generally considered to be the greatest of all the prophets, does not have any books in the Old Testament. In fact, most of the prophets mentioned in historical accounts have no published works. This does not mean they are unimportant, simply unpublished.

PROPHETS OF THE LORD

While there is a strong aspect of prediction in prophecy, Bible prophets do not exist simply to foretell the future. Their visions serve to underscore the main message of moral reform—the goal is to eradicate sin. Prophets are often royal advisers, but most are found working among the common people.

JONAH, RELUCTANT PROPHET TO HIS ENEMIES

It's hard to talk about Jonah the prophet without mentioning the giant fish. Jonah's story, it seems, will be forever tied to the beast that swallows him.

Jonah and the Whale by Pieter Lastman (ca. 1610)

A LIST OF SOME PROMINENT PROPHETS

PROPHET	AUDIENCE	MESSAGE/MISSION
Elijah	Primarily Ahab	Eradicates Baal worship
Elisha	Populous of Israel, but often political leaders both foreign and domestic	Focuses on personal moral accountability
Joel	Judah	Makes comparisons between a devastating locust plague and the coming invasion of the Babylonians
Hosea	Israel	Marries an unfaithful prostitute, Gomer, as a living testimony of Israel's unfaithfulness to God
Isaiah	Judah and surrounding nations	Concentrates on the judgments pronounced on Judah and the surrounding nations
Micah	Judah and Israel	Preaches the Lord's coming judgment; describes exile of the nations, and eventual restoration
Jeremiah	Judah	Addresses political and social concerns from a religious point of view
Jonah	Israel and Assyria	Preaches the impending doom of Assyria
Ezekiel	Judean exiles	Offers visions of world history and the Lord's ultimate triumph
Daniel	Judean exiles	Admonishes exiles to work on the restoration of the temple
Haggai	Returning Judean exiles	Brief admonition to work on the restoration of the temple quickly
Zechariah	Returning Judean exiles	Apocalyptic treatment of restoration

Legend   Unpublished   Major   Minor

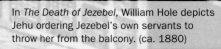
In *The Death of Jezebel*, William Hole depicts Jehu ordering Jezebel's own servants to throw her from the balcony. (ca. 1880)

2 KINGS 9–25; 2 CHRONICLES 25–36

Collapse of the Kingdoms

ISRAEL FALLS FIRST. BUT
JUDAH IS NOT SPARED.

After the death of Joash, a number of ineffectual kings preside over Israel's spiritual decline. The era is marked by idol worship, violence, and instability until the kingdom finally is forced into exile by Assyria around 723 B.C.

Judah experiences a national revival. The high point of religious change comes under the reign of Hezekiah, who restores temple worship, the observance of Passover, and many other sacred customs. The revival lasts until the emperor Nebuchadnezzar takes Judah captive to Babylon around 586 B.C.

THE END OF THE KINGS

The dizzying succession of kings chronicles two spiritual paths, intended to provide lessons to the people. The account in 1 and 2 Kings shows a contrast between the universally evil kings of the north and the typically good kings of the south. The moral rectitude of the southern kings is what allows Judah to exist for more than a century after Israel's fall.

Chronicles gives a far more detailed account of the Judean kings. As long as they honor the traditions of their fathers, they do well. But when they stop praying to the Lord and sully their worship with pagan practices, the kingdom finally falls.

Both Kings and Chronicles stand as object lessons of God's faithfulness to those who honor him.

King Hezekiah in the church of
Sankta Maria Kyrka, Åhus, Sweden,
by an unknown artist (17th century)

A relief thought to have been found in King Nebuchadnezzar's hanging garden in Babylon (604–562 B.C.). The ancient glazed ceramic tiles depict a lion, the symbol of Babylon, and represent Ishtar, the goddess of fertility, love, and war.

CHAPTER 7

JUDAH IS EXILED AND RETURNED

The Babylonians conquer the Kingdom of Judah, destroy Jerusalem, and around 598 B.C., King Nebuchadnezzar orders the deportation of the Jews. This marks the beginning of the Babylonia Exile.

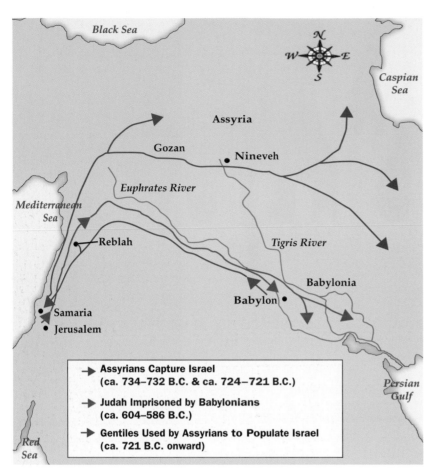

The Destruction of Jerusalem
by Louis Haghe (ca. 1840)

Map legend:
- → Assyrians Capture Israel
  (ca. 734–732 B.C. & ca. 724–721 B.C.)
- → Judah Imprisoned by Babylonians
  (ca. 604–586 B.C.)
- → Gentiles Used by Assyrians to Populate Israel
  (ca. 721 B.C. onward)

▲ Map showing the routes the nations Israel and Judah take during their exiles.

WHAT IS A LAMENT?
Written during Israel's captivity in Babylon, Psalm 137 is a lament or a passionate expression of sorrow. In this case, the lament is for the disobedience that led to Israel's captivity in Babylon and for the destruction of Israel.

Basic structure of Psalm 137:
- Verses 1–4: Lament
- Verses 5–6: Confession of trust
- Verses 7–9: Petition or request of God

1 CHRONICLES
Life in Captivity

THE EXILE FORCES THE JEWISH PEOPLE TO EMBRACE THEIR FAITH.

When Judah's ruler Zedekiah decides to withhold annual taxes from the empire, the Babylonian king, Nebuchadnezzar, orders the invasion of Judah and the decimation of Jerusalem. He sends the Jews into exile, the first time in at least 600 years that there is no nation of Judah. Taken from their homeland and stripped of their national identity, the Judeans rally around the only thing they have left that maintains their identity as a people—their sacred traditions.

During this period, the Jews concentrate on their spiritual lives. The devotion that helped Jacob's descendants survive in Egypt before the Exodus, refined by a millennium of experience, serves them well during this dark time and makes their restoration possible.

It will be 50 years before they return home.

> **Psalm 137:1-3**
> By the rivers of Babylon—
>   there we sat down and there we wept
>   when we remembered Zion.
> On the willows
>   there we hung up our harps.
> For there our captors
>   asked us for songs,
> and our tormentors asked for mirth, saying,
>   "Sing us one of the songs of Zion!"

TIMELINE OF THE EXILE AND RESTORATION

DATE (B.C.)	SECULAR RULER	
606–562	Nebuchadnezzar	Events in Daniel 1–4, including the fall of Jerusalem; deportation of Jews to Babylon; and destruction of the temple
562–560	Evil-merodach	Release of Jehoiachin from prison
556–539	Nabonidus Belshazzar	Events in Daniel 5, including the conquest of Babylon by the Medo-Persians
539–522	Cyrus Cambyses	Events in Ezra 1–3, including the return of first exiles to Jerusalem and the beginning of the rebuilding of the temple
521–486	Darius the Great	Second decree to rebuild the temple Events in Ezra 6–10, including the end of construction and dedication of the Temple
485–465	Ahasuerus	Events in the Book of Esther, including the banishment of Vashti; the rise of Esther as queen; and the foiling of Haman's plan to destroy the Jews
465–424	Artaxerxes I	Events in the Book of Nehemiah, including the return of exiles under governorship of Nehemiah and the rebuilding of the wall around Jerusalem

Legend   ▇ Babylonian Empire   ▇ Persian Empire

Shadrach, Meshach and Abednego in the Fiery Furnace by an unknown artist (1863)

Daniel's Answer to the King
by Briton Rivière (1890)

DANIEL, ESTHER
Living Apart
GOD CALLS PROPHETS TO GUIDE
THE ISRAELITES IN CAPTIVITY.

While the Israelites are in exile in Babylon, King Nebuchadnezzar brings selected captives back to the kingdom to serve as liaisons between the subjugated peoples and the imperial court. Typically, he chooses the juvenile survivors of royal households for the task.

Daniel, Hananiah, Mishael, and Azariah are summoned to be schooled in the local language, in court manners, and in governmental administration. Daniel is renamed Belteshazzar; Hananiah becomes Shadrach; Mishael is Meshach; and Azariah becomes Abednego.

The four students win favor with the school administration, but that position is threatened when they refuse to eat meat from the imperial table because it isn't kosher. The men pass a performance trial while on their diet and are permitted to follow their dietary customs.

Throughout their service to the court, Belteshazzar, Shadrach, Meshach, and Abednego continue to fight for their traditions. In one instance, when they refuse to bow to an idol, Nebuchadnezzar threatens to burn them to death. God intervenes and protects the four from the fire, prompting the king to allow the Jews to pray as they wish.

DANIEL IN THE LION'S DEN
With the fall of the Babylonian Empire and the establishment of the Persian Empire, however, some of the customs are revoked. In defiance of an imperial edict, Daniel, an old man by this time, continues to pray daily to God. As punishment, he is imprisoned in a den of Asiatic lions. When an angel intervenes, Daniel is spared and the advisers who promoted the royal law are fed to the lions instead. Daniel is permitted to continue his customary prayers.

▲ *Daniel Interprets the Writing on the Wall* by an unknown artist

▲ *Daniel Stands Before King Nebuchadnezzar* by an unknown artist

DANIEL
Daniel's Dreams and Visions

GOD GIVES THE YOUNG PROPHET AN AMAZING ABILITY.

The Book of Daniel contains a stunning series of visions, each one providing a detailed view of history. Here they are, presented in the same order as the Hebrew Bible.

- **Nebuchadnezzar's Image:** Daniel sees a statue that he says represents a succession of kingdoms. It's head is of gold, symbolizing Nebuchadnezzar. The statue's other body parts are fashioned from silver, bronze, iron, and clay, indicating rulers who will succeed Nebuchadnezzar.
- **Handwriting on the Wall:** Daniel describes a hand that writes on the palace wall in an unknown language during a feast of Belshazzar, the last king of Babylon. Daniel interprets the writing and the meaning as announcing the fall of the Babylonian kingdom.
- **Creatures from the Sea:** In a dream, Daniel sees four animals emerging from a body of water: a lion, a bear, a leopard, and an unidentified beast with iron teeth and ten horns. Daniel interprets this to mean four kingdoms, which scholars believe represent Babylon, Persia, Greece, and Rome. The dream is thought by scholars to foreshadow the rise of God as ruler of the Earth.
- **Ram and the Goat:** Daniel dreams of a ram that is attacked and killed by a goat with a conspicuous horn. The horn then splits into four unique horns that grow toward the four corners of the Earth. This passage has been interpreted by scholars as representing the defeat of the Persian empire under its first king by the Greeks and the division of the kingdom into four.
- **Seventy Weeks:** One of the most controversial visions in the Book of Daniel, this dream involves the rebuilding of the temple, reestablishment of sacrificial worship, the coming and destruction of "an anointed one," and the subsequent destruction of the city and the temple. The timing and meaning of these events are widely disputed among various Jewish and Christian traditions. Some see the "anointed one" as Cyrus; others think it refers to Jesus.
- **Kings of the South and the North:** Chapters 10–12 of Daniel contain a complicated story of conflicts between the kings of the north and the kings of the south. The passages often are interpreted by scholars as a prophecy of the wars between the Selucid kings in Asia Minor and the Ptolemy kings in Egypt. Some think the chapters predict the rise of Rome under Mark Antony and Cleopatra.

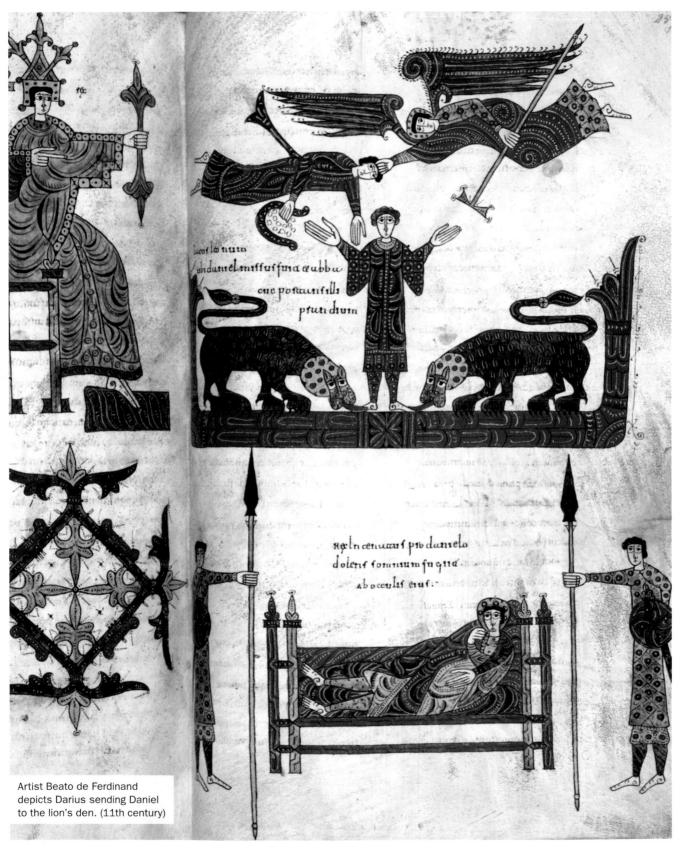

luauf lco num
ubi dum el miffuf fna æ ubb a
cue poscuin filli
p tun diuin

rægi In cenuaui p ro daniclo
dolenf fomnium fu quia
ab occulif cruf.

Artist Beato de Ferdinand depicts Darius sending Daniel to the lion's den. (11th century)

▲ Esther risks her life by entering the throne room of the king unbidden in *Esther and Ahasuerus*, by an unknown artist. (ca. 1775)

ESTHER
A Jewish Queen

THE YOUNG PROPHET RISKS
HER LIFE FOR HER PEOPLE.

During this period of exile, Ahasuerus becomes the king of Persia in Babylon. Three years into his rule, Ahasuerus hosts a banquet and commands his queen, Vashti, to appear in front of his male guests. Vashti refuses, prompting Ahasuerus to banish her. He orders his officials to bring the most beautiful young women of the kingdom into his harem so they he may choose a replacement.

Mordecai, a palace functionary and Jew, suggests to his cousin Hadassah that she present herself to the keeper of the harem as "Esther" (meaning "Star") but that she keep her religion secret. Esther is not only taken into the harem, she becomes the king's favorite and is appointed queen.

Soon, Mordecai foils a plot to assassinate the king and rises in the palace ranks until he crosses Haman, Ahasuerus's highest official. By refusing to bow to

Brave Queen Esther Accuses Haman in this illustration by Arthur Dixon. (ca. 1915)

Haman, Mordecai infuriates the king's aide and becomes the subject of a plot himself. Learning that Mordecai is a Jew, Haman convinces Ahasuerus to order the extermination of all Jews in the kingdom. The slaughter date is set a year ahead, so that Haman will have time to execute the plan.

ESTHER RISKS HER LIFE

Within a short time, Mordecai persuades Esther to intercede and save her people. She does so at the risk of her own life, by entering the king's presence unbidden and inviting Ahasuerus and Haman to a series of dinners. On the second day of feasting, Esther reveals that Haman has tricked the king into signing a decree that will result in her death and in the death of all Jews. Enraged, the king orders Haman to be hanged on the gallows that were custom-built for Mordecai.

Yet even with Haman gone, Ahasuerus cannot rescind his decree. Instead, he issues a counter-proclamation calling for the Jews to take up arms and defend themselves from any who would execute the king's original order, thus rescuing the Jewish people from annihilation. The Jews rejoice at their change in fortune.

THE FEAST OF PURIM

This holiday is a way for Jews to remember and celebrate the bravery of Queen Esther and how the Jews fought against their enemies and won.

During the Purim service, it is customary to boo and hiss whenever the name of Haman is mentioned.

Many Jews celebrate Purim by exchanging gifts, eating special foods, drinking wine, and wearing masks and costumes.

▲ *Cyrus the Great Leads Successful Conquest of Babylon* by an unknown artist

King Cyrus Restores the Vessels to the Temple by Gustave Doré (1865)

WHO'S WHO?

- **King Cyrus** was the king of Persia who gave the Edict of Restoration—the right of the Jews to return to their lands.
- **Artaxerxes** was the Persian king who sent Ezra first, and Nehemiah later, to Jerusalem to restore the temple.

Life Back Home

A SCRIBE AND A LEADER WORK
TO REBUILD THE TEMPLE.

Just as the exile into Babylon occurs in successive waves over the course of several years, so too does the Israelites' return and restoration to their lands.

The restoration of the Israelites to Judea is ordered by King Cyrus of Persia in 538 B.C., a time of religious and political turmoil in Jerusalem. While the Israelites have been in exile, some of their ancestral enemies have ascended to power, and the landscape has changed. Many of the area's poor and peasant farmers left behind are suffering.

CLASH OF CULTURES

In Samaria, the area around the former capital of the northern kingdom of Israel, foreigners have intermarried with the Jews who were not taken into exile. The Samaritans, as they are called, consider themselves followers of the Jewish faith. The returning exiles, however, reject them and do not accept them as Jews.

Another issue the returning exiles face is who speaks locally for the civil authority back in Babylon. Who, in other words, has

power to settle land disputes, enact and enforce laws, and develop a military?

All of these developments represent a menace to Judean autonomy on a civil level or a threat to religious purity (and their spiritual identity) on a sacred level.

Much of what is contained in the post-exilic writings has to do with establishing and maintaining spiritual purity as a means of securing their national and ethnic identity.

APPROXIMATE DATES OF RETURN AND RESTORATION

- **538 B.C.** – The *Cyrus Declaration* ends the exile of Jews in Babylon and permits their return to Israel. Jews to return to land of Judah.
- **536 B.C.** – Temple restoration begins in Jerusalem.
- **520 B.C.** – Return of exiles under Zerubbabel and Jeshua
- **445 B.C.** – Nehemiah returns to Jerusalem and embarks on rebuilding the wall of the city.

▲ *Ezra Reading the Torah*, illustration from *L'Histoire Sainte*, Paris (late 19th century)

Julius Schnorr von Carolsfeld depicts the laying of the foundation stone for the temple in Jerusalem. (late 19th century)

VERSE TO KNOW

"Thus says King Cyrus of Persia: The Lord, the God of heaven, has given me all the kingdoms of the earth, and he has charged me to build him a house at Jerusalem in Judah." (Ezra 1:2)

Ezra and Nehemiah

BOTH MEN WORK TO RESTORE THE WORSHIP OF GOD IN A RESTORED TEMPLE.

Ezra is a scribe during the reign of Artaxerxes whose book chronicles the first two phases of the return from exile.

Chapters 1–6 of Ezra describe how King Cyrus commissions the rebuilding of the temple in Jerusalem and sends Zerubbabel, a governor in the Persian province of Judah, and Jeshua the High Priest, to lead a first contingent of exiles back to the land. These leaders start the work of rebuildng the altar and reinstitute the observance of Sukkot (the Feast of Tabernacles).

The Samaritans and other local inhabitants, alarmed by the return of the Israelites, challenge the work of Zerubbabel and Jeshua and write to the king to bring construction to a halt. After some negotiations, Cyrus's emissaries are allowed to continue their work.

In chapters 7–10, Artaxerxes commissions Ezra to appoint officials to administer justice to the returning exiles. The scribe and a large number of Israelites leave for Jerusalem, taking with them vast wealth to use in the service of the Lord. Upon returning, Ezra discovers that some recent arrivals have married local non-Jewish

women. Disturbed by the interfaith marriages, Ezra confronts the offenders and orders them to send away their foreign wives and children.

NEHEMIAH

Nehemiah, an official to the Persian court, is appointed governor of Judea by Artaxerxes and is sent to Jerusalem to administer justice to the people in the emperor's name.

Upon arrival, Nehemiah inspects the walls of the city and finds them in hopeless disrepair. He commissions a workforce to begin fortifying Jerusalem. Because of interference by some local people, the work proceeds slowly. Eventually, Nehemiah arms the workers and they are able to complete the work of building the city walls.

As governor, Nehemiah institutes both civil and religious reforms including tax relief, elimination of the governor's stipend, cronyism, and the cancellation of debts and mortgages. He also calls for a public reading of the Torah by Ezra and the reestablishment of the traditional feasts under the direction of a rededicated priesthood.

After 12 years of improvements, Nehemiah returns to the Persian capital in Susa.

Time passes, and Nehemiah hears that the priest Eliashib has installed his family in richly appointed apartments of the temple instead of using the facilities to help the Levites. He gets permission from Artaxerxes to return and, when he arrives, stops the corrupt practices.

▲ A relief of Xerxes, a descendent of Cyrus, at the ancient doorway of Xerxes's palace in Persepolis, Iran (460 B.C.)

▲ *The Cyrus Cylinder*, found in the ruins of Babylon, Iraq, in 1879, is a clay cylinder written in Akkadian cuneiform script around 539 B.C. It lists the genealogy of King Cyrus.

▲ *The Vision of the Prophet Ezekiel of the Rising of the Dead* by Quentin Massys (1507)

Enter the Prophets

CALLING THE PEOPLE TO BE BETTER

For the most part, the prophets who minister during and after the exile focus on moral reform. They support the work of Ezra and Nehemiah through their calls for spiritual purity. In addition to delivering messages from God, the prophets see the future and help spark social change.

- **Isaiah:** Lists judgments pronounced on Judah for ethical lapses along with promises of restoration.
- **Jeremiah:** Foresees the coming siege of Jerusalem and the destruction of the temple.
- **Ezekiel:** Describes skeletal remains coming to life and growing flesh and skin, representing the restoration of Israel to nationhood.
- **Hosea:** Illustrates God's compassion.

Angels Driving Chariots in Zechariah's Vision by an unknown artist (1754)

▲ *The Statue of the Prophet Jeremiah* by Aleijadinho at the Basilica do Bom Jesus de Matosinhos, Congonhas, Brazil (ca. 18th century)

- **Joel:** Predicts a terrible judgment day, but also offers hope if the people return to God.
- **Amos:** Compares a devastating locust plague and the coming invasion of the Babylonians.
- **Obadiah:** Criticizes the kingdom of Edom, which has retreated to the security of their fortified cities.
- **Jonah:** Asks forgiveness from God, but does not extend it to others.
- **Micah:** Denounces social evils and foresees peace through obedience.
- **Nahum:** Poetically addresses the destruction of Nineveh.
- **Habakkuk:** Argues with the Lord for using the wicked Babylonians as instruments of judgment against the chosen people.

- **Zephaniah:** Briefly describes the Great Day of the Lord and the impending Babylonian captivity.
- **Haggai:** Admonishes the people to not waver in the rebuilding of the temple.
- **Zechariah:** Through apocalyptic visions, provides a foundation for some familiar motifs in the New Testament Book of Revelation.
- **Malachi:** Gives impassioned pleas for religious reform in the last book in the Old Testament. In the closing text, God promises that the faithful will be rewarded and warns that Elijah will return to punish the wicked. "He will turn the hearts of parents to their children and the hearts of children to their parents, so that I will not come and strike the land with a curse." **(Malachi 4:6)**

THE WEEPING PROPHET
The prophet Jeremiah is called "the weeping prophet" because of the profound grief he experiences when the Jewish people rebuff his efforts to turn them away from sin, back to God, and to warn them of the coming exile.

THE DEAD SEA SCROLLS

Copies of the Bible from the early Christian era had existed for millennia, but there were no known examples of the Torah or the Old Testament from the time of Jesus. In the spring of 1947, that changed when a shepherd stumbled upon some clay jars in a cave near Qumran along the Dead Sea in Israel.

The jars discovered by the herdsman had lain in the cave for almost two millennia and contained sections of the Hebrew Bible dating from the 300s B.C. to 70 A.D. The scrolls had been preserved by the dry, salty climate around the Dead Sea, but only to a certain extent. Most of the manuscripts were in tiny pieces, and as scholars and locals searched other caves in the area over the next nine years, they found remnants of 972 manuscripts in 15,000 fragments.

In all, one complete Torah, or the first five books of the Old Testament, were found in the scrolls, as well as fragments of every book in the Hebrew Bible, except Esther. One scroll held the Psalms, including some that were previously unknown. Others contained Jewish hymns and prayers, as well as philosophical works unique to the Essenes, the Jewish sect believed to have stored their holy scrolls in the cave after a disagreement with religious leaders in Jerusalem. One scroll described how the ideal temple of Jerusalem should be constructed.

Besides being a wonderful find for archaeologists and historians, the Dead Sea Scrolls reshaped how biblical scholars thought about the Jewish world. The scrolls and their location proved that there was not one monolithic Jewish faith during the first century B.C. but rather many different groups. The scrolls helped better understand the faith and the world into which Jesus was born.

One of the five caves where the Scrolls were found

LANGUAGES
The Scrolls were written in a variety of scripts, including Hebrew, Aramaic, Greek, Latin, and Nabataean, a variation on the pre-Arabic alphabet.

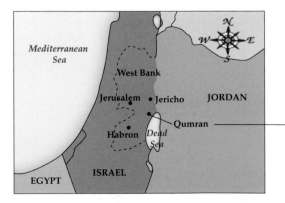

NUMBERING
Archaeologists coded each manuscript to signify where it was unearthed and what it contained. For example, "11QPsalms" was found in Cave 1 at Qumran, and featured Psalm 133.

MATERIALS
Manuscripts found were written on papyrus, leather, and even copper.

VALUE
In the 1950s, an archaeologist bought two fairly complete scrolls for a mere $324. In recent years, small fragments have sold for $35 million or more.

SITES
The Scrolls were discovered at five different sites around the Dead Sea, including one cave near Jericho. There, Samarian legal documents were uncovered along with the bodies of 205 people who were probably killed in 331 B.C. by soldiers of Alexander the Great.

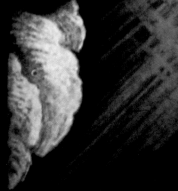

CHAPTER 8

JESUS: THE EARLY YEARS

One of the greatest figures in history grows up in humble circumstances with his family in Nazareth. He works with his father as a carpenter and develops a deep understanding of Hebrew scriptures before leaving home at 30 to begin his ministry.

Four Answers to an Eternally Compelling Question

THE GOSPELS TELL US MOST OF WHAT WE NOW ABOUT THE SON OF GOD.

▲ The opening passage of the Gospel of Mark, from the *Bible of Borso d'Este* was illuminated by Taddeo Crivelli (1425–1479). The manuscript is from the collection of the Biblioteca Estense in Modena, Italy.

Who exactly was Jesus? Each of the four Gospel writers has his own unique approach to answering this question.

- **Matthew** (also called Levi, former tax collector and apostle) focuses on Jesus as king and Messiah. Writing for his fellow Jews who are familiar with the Old Testament, Matthew fills his Gospel with Old Testament messianic prophecies that are fulfilled in Jesus's life. He begins by tracing Jesus's legal bloodline through his adopted father Joseph back to Abraham. This genealogy is unusual because, in addition to Mary, it includes Ruth, a Gentile, plus three women who committed sexual sin: Tamar, Rahab, and Bathsheba.

- **Mark** (collaborated with Peter and Paul and founded the church of Africa) writes the shortest and most action-packed Gospel, probably intended for a Roman audience. He emphasizes Jesus as a suffering servant. Some believe Mark is the naked streaker who runs away when Jesus is arrested. **(14:51-52)**

- **Luke** (Gentile physician and companion of Paul) is the only Gospel writer who didn't know Jesus personally. Instead, Luke carefully compiles his account through investigation and interviews with individuals who spent time with Christ, such as his mother, Mary. Luke focuses on Jesus's parables, teachings, and miracles. He writes what most scholars believe is Jesus's biological genealogy, starting with Mary and reaching back to forebears such as David and Adam.

- **John** (former fisherman and part of Jesus's inner circle of disciples) completes his Gospel about 30 years later than the other writers, so his approach is quite different. John mentions seven miracles but focuses on the ones that show Jesus is God's Son—such as the episode in which Jesus raises Lazarus from the dead. **(11:1-44)** John's Gospel includes a famous Bible verse:

  "For God so loved the world that he gave his only Son, so that everyone who believes in him may not perish but may have eternal life." **(3:16)**

DID JESUS REALLY EXIST?

Most modern secular scholars of antiquity agree that Jesus lived, though they differ on how historically accurate the biblical accounts of his life are.

The early writer Josephus (A.D. 37-100) refers to Jesus as "a wise man" who did "amazing deeds" and states that he was executed by Pontius Pilate. Tacitus (A.D. 56-117), a great Roman historian, writes about "Christus," who died at the hands of Pilate.

The Holy Family with Saint Elizabeth (right), Saint John the Baptist (kneeling in front), and two angels, by Anton Raphael Mengs (1749)

WHY IS THE BIRTH OF JOHN SO SIGNIFICANT?

John has an important assignment, as foretold by his father: "And you, child, will be called the prophet of the Most High; for you will go before the Lord to prepare his ways." (Luke 1:76, 77) His life task: to ready the world for the coming Messiah.

THE MARY DEBATES

Christian communities around the world venerate Mary, the Jewish woman from Nazareth who gave birth to Jesus.

But there is sharp theological debate about Mary's role beyond physically delivering the Son of God.

Some Protestants, including most Evangelicals, see Mary simply as the mother of Jesus, and her role is limited to her giving him physical birth. Other traditions, such as Catholics, Orthodox, and Copts, believe that since Mary was the mother of Jesus, she was also the Mother of God—the Theotokos or the bearer of God. These communities have developed theologies and practices specifically around Mary, such as Catholics saying the Rosary—a sacramental prayer that honors her.

MATTHEW 1; LUKE 1, 2

A World of Wonder

THE AMAZING BIRTH OF JOHN IS FOLLWED BY THE MIRACULOUS ARRIVAL OF BABY JESUS.

A period of 400 years passes without prophets or miracles. Then, incredible events begin occurring again, starting with births to two unlikely couples in Judea, a client-kingdom of Rome:: an elderly priest and his barren wife and a young virgin and her fiancé.

HERALDING A BOY NAMED JOHN

It is the angel Gabriel who signals the new era with two prophecies. First, he appears to the old priest Zechariah and tells him that his wife, Elizabeth, will soon bear a son and that the couple is to call the baby John. Zechariah doubts the angel's words and is struck dumb, but Elizabeth does conceive and give birth as prophesized. Zechariah miraculously recovers his voice only when he writes on a tablet, "His name is John."

A VIRGIN IS STARTLED

But another even more amazing birth is about to take place. This time, Gabriel appears to Mary, a young virgin. She is startled when the angel tells her she is favored by God and will become pregnant and give birth to a son to be called "Son of the Most High." Mary asks how this will be possible, since she is a virgin. Gabriel explains that the Holy Spirit will come upon her and overshadow her, so that the child will be called the Son of God. Mary accepts Gabriel's words and says,

"Here am I, the servant of the Lord . . ."

Although distressed to learn his young fiancée is pregnant, and not by him, Joseph takes Mary as his wife when an angel tells him,

"Do not be afraid to take Mary as your wife, for the child conceived in her is from the Holy Spirit."

The Nativity at Night, by Guido Reni (1640)

WHAT'S IN A NAME?
Jesus in Greek means the same as *Joshua* in Hebrew. *Joshua* and *Jesus* translate to: "God is salvation."

ONE NEWBORN, MANY INTERPRETATIONS

For some, the birth of Jesus is seen as the fulfillment of an Old Testament prophecy that a virgin would conceive and have a son. (Isaiah 7:14) For others, the virgin birth is proof that Jesus was both fully human (child of Mary) and fully divine (Son of God). A third school holds that the birth is evidence that God sent his Son into history as Jesus, who will *"save his people from their sins."* (Matthew 1:21)

DO THE MATH

How is it possible Jesus Christ is born four to six years B.C. (In other words, before Christ)? In the 6th century, the Greek historian Dionysius proposed making the birth of Jesus the basis of the calendar, and labeled years after the birth Anno Domini, or A.D. However, he miscalculated the year Herod died, which we now know was 4 B.C. John's and Jesus's births would have occurred before that, so the calendar is off by four to six years.

APPROXIMATE TIMELINE

Birth of John the Baptist	6-5 B.C.
Birth of Jesus (six months later)	6-4 B.C.
Death of Herod the Great	4 B.C.

A young woman attempts to flee Herod's soldiers in
Antonio Puccinelli's *The Massacre of the Innocents.* (1852)

LUKE 2; MATTHEW 2

Angels, Shepherds, Wise Men, and a Wicked King

THE STORY OF CHRIST'S BIRTH READS LIKE A THRILLER, WITH DEATH THREATS AND A MIDNIGHT ESCAPE.

Only two Gospels—Matthew and Luke—discuss Jesus's birth, and the amazing events they record are fitting for a newborn king and Savior.

BRIGHT ANGELS ON A DARK NIGHT

Luke's account of angels appearing to shepherds on the night of Jesus's birth gives early clues of who Jesus will become. The first angel says,

"Do not be afraid; for see—I am bringing you good news of great joy for all the people: to you is born this day in the city of David a Savior, who is the Messiah, the Lord."

Then a host of angels fills the sky, singing glory to God. When the angels leave, the shepherds hurry into town and find the baby as described. After viewing him with wonder, they spread the news of all they have seen and heard.

VISITORS FOLLOW A STAR FROM AFAR

Some foreign astrologers, known as Magi or Wise Men, spot an unusual star in the sky. Instinctively, they know a king of the Jews has been born, and they follow the star to Jerusalem, the capital, as the most likely birthplace. The Magi visit the local king Herod to ask about this omen. Herod is frightened by the prospect of a new king coming to replace him, and he asks the Magi to return with news after they find the baby. Herod claims he wants to pay his respects to the new king of the Jews, but his real plan is to murder the child.

VERSE TO KNOW
"I am bringing you good news of great joy for all the people: to you is born this day in the city of David a Savior, who is the Messiah, the Lord." **(Luke 2:10-11)**

Warned in a dream of the deception, the Magi follow the star to the exact location of Jesus's family. They honor the new king with gifts of great value: gold, special incense used for worship, and myrrh, or oil used for burial. After delivering these gifts, the Magi continue their journey, but do *not* return to Herod.

ESCAPE FROM DEATH

Herod the Great is enraged when the Wise Men fail to return to tell him where to find the baby. He orders all the baby boys under the age of two in Bethlehem killed, but Jesus escapes because an angel tells Joseph to take his family and flee to Egypt.

▲ *The Adoration of the Magi* by Geertgen tot Sint Jans (15th century)

NEWS FOR ALL
In announcing the birth of Jesus, why do the angels appear to lowly shepherds, instead of priests and scholars? One theory is that God's good news is for all, not just for the elite. The story is only the second in the Bible where a group, rather than a single angel is depicted. The first instance is in Genesis 28, when Jacob sees a flock of angels ascending and descending a ladder to heaven.

EXTRA SPECIAL DELIVERY
Were the Magi present at the manger? While most nativity scenes include three kings bearing gifts, these travelers probably arrive months after the actual birth. Matthew clues us in with this passage describing their first encounter with Jesus: "On entering the house, they saw the child with Mary his mother." **(Matthew 2:11)** Since Jesus is already a child, some time has passed since his birth.

APPROXIMATE TIMELINE

Shepherds visit the newborn baby Jesus	6-4 B.C.
Visit of the Magi (months later)	5-4 B.C.
Herod's slaughter of the baby boys	5-4 B.C.

MY FATHER

Why does Jesus refer to God as his father? While Joseph functions as a parent on a human level, Jesus early on distinguishes between Joseph and God. His statement indicates he is aware that his relationship with God is unique.

PURE WATER

Was John's baptismal ceremony something new? Jews were used to baptism as a cleansing ritual, submerging themselves in water and repeating the practice as needed for purification. Both John's method and motive are different. He submerges believers in the water and lifts them out again only once. Participants—still Jewish—first repent their sins and then are forgiven.

APPROXIMATE TIMELINE

Jesus meets with the teachers in the temple	A.D. 6-8
John the Baptist begins his ministry	A.D. 24-26

MATTHEW 3; MARK 1; LUKE 2, 3

Special Years

EVEN AS A YOUNG BOY, JESUS HAS A UNIQUE RELATIONSHIP WITH GOD.

Jesus and John grow up separately, but each is preparing for the time when their lives will intersect.

LOSING JESUS

Each year for Passover, it is Mary and Joseph's custom to travel to Jerusalem to celebrate the holiday.

When Jesus is 12, they make the trip as usual, but once it has ended and they are on their way home, Joseph and Mary discover that Jesus has disappeared from the caravan.

They return to Jerusalem, search for three days, and finally find Jesus in the temple. He's sitting in the middle of Israel's foremost scholars, listening intently and asking searching questions. The holy men, experts in Hebrew scriptures, are amazed at the depth of understanding in one so young.

When Mary asks Jesus why he disappeared, he answers her,

"Why were you searching for me? Did you not know that I must be in my Father's house?"

Having said that, he returns home with them to Nazareth.

A NORMAL FAMILY LIFE

Jesus grows up living a quiet life with his family in Nazareth. He has four younger half-brothers and several half-sisters, according to Matthew (13:55-56), although Catholics believe they were cousins. Since Joseph is a carpenter, Jesus learns the trade and works on projects typical of the time, such as making yokes and building furniture."

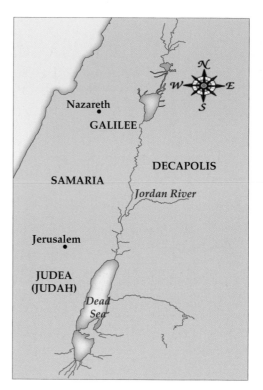

▲ Jesus was born in Bethlehem, a town in the region of Judea. At that time, the region was ruled by the Romans, who had set up King Herod as a puppet ruler.

JOHN BECOMES "THE BAPTIST"

Before the start of his public ministry, John can be found with his elderly parents Zachariah and Elizabeth in Ein Karem, a village near Jerusalem. John and Jesus are related through their mothers, Elizabeth and Mary, who are cousins.

At about age 30, John moves to the wilderness of Judea, close to the Jordan River, so he can fulfill his God-given mission.

With his long, uncut hair, powerful voice, strange attire, and compelling call to repent, John attracts streams of listeners as he delivers his message. Many people respond and want to be cleansed of their sins, and John proceeds to baptize them in the Jordan.

At the same time, he begins to alert the crowds that the Messiah will be appearing soon.

Jesus With the Doctors by Augustin Theodule Ribot (ca. 19th century)

John Baptizes Jesus

THE BEGINNING OF A PUBLIC MINISTRY

Jesus's baptism, which is found in all four Gospels, is a turning point for him and the beginning of his ministry. But, how did it happen, and why?

- **The How:** At age 30, knowing it's time to begin his vocation, Jesus leaves Nazareth and heads to the Jordan River where John is baptizing people. When John sees Jesus, he protests:

  "I need to be baptized by you, and do you come to me?"

  Jesus reassures him it is important to meet all of God's requirements. John agrees to perform the rite, and Jesus enters the Jordan River.

  After Jesus is baptized, he and John see Heaven torn apart as the Holy Spirit descends in the form of a dove. When the bird lights on Jesus, a voice from Heaven speaks:

  "This is my Son, the Beloved, with whom I am well pleased."

- **The Why:** For some, the baptism signifies the Spirit descending on Jesus, God identifying Jesus as his Son, and God approving of Jesus and his ministry.

  Others believe Jesus allows John to baptize him in order for Jesus to be able to identify with sinful humans and to set an example.

  In John 1:32-34, God informs the Baptist he will know the Messiah when he sees the Holy Spirit come down on him.

  From this moment on, John openly declares that Jesus is the Messiah.

EXPLAINING THE RITE

Baptism, a central ritual in Christianity, consists of two parts. In the first, the person being baptized comes in contact with or is immersed in water. In the second, there is a pronouncement: "I baptize you in the name of the Father, Son, and Holy Spirit." Depending on the faith tradition, baptism does some or all for the believer:

- commemorates Christ's death and resurrection
- fulfills the command of Jesus to baptize
- cleanses away sins
- confers grace
- publicly expresses one's faith
- grants the baptized person rights to full participation in a faith community

VERSE TO KNOW

"The Spirit immediately drove him out into the wilderness. He was in the wilderness forty days, tempted by Satan . . ." **(Mark 1:12-13)**

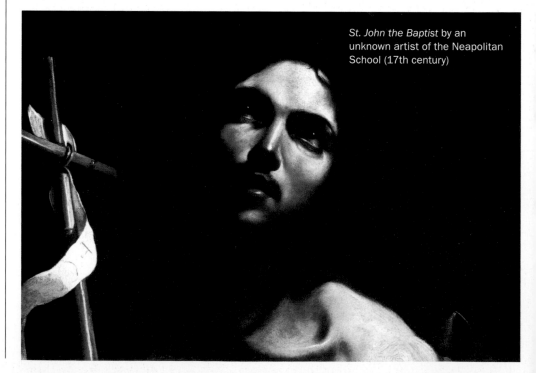

St. John the Baptist by an unknown artist of the Neapolitan School (17th century)

John baptizes Jesus in Francesco Trevisani's *The Baptism of Christ*. (1723)

MATTHEW 4:1-11; MARK 1:12-13; LUKE 4:1-13

Resisting Temptation

SATAN TAUNTS JESUS THREE TIMES BUT IS
UNABLE TO BREAK THE SON OF GOD.

From the beginning of Jesus's ministry, Satan, his supernatural adversary, challenges and battles him. In this section, he encounters Jesus in the wilderness where he has undertaken a 40-day fast, and tries three different temptations. Jesus however triumphs with a powerful weapon: the Holy Scriptures.

Turn Stones to Bread: Satan tempts Jesus throughout the fast, but he waits until Jesus is truly starving to taunt:

"If you are the Son of God, command these stones to become loaves of bread."

Instead of seeking to execute the task, Jesus replies that one doesn't live by bread alone but by the word of God.

Be Caught by Angels: The devil then takes Jesus to the highest point of the temple. As Jesus looks at the 100-foot drop, Satan says, "If you are the Son of God, throw yourself down," and angels will you catch you. Again Jesus refuses and quotes Scripture, saying,

"Do not put the Lord your God to the test."

Bow and Worship Me: In a miraculous vision, Satan shows Jesus the glory of the world's kingdoms. Then he says,

"To you I will give their glory and all this authority; for it has been given over to me, and I give it to anyone I please. If you, then, will worship me, it will all be yours."

Jesus responds by dismissing the devil:

"Away with you, Satan! for it is written, 'Worship the Lord your God, and serve only him.'"

Angels then surround Jesus, and Satan retreats to bide his time and hope for a rematch.

Jesus Tempted by Satan
by Mattia Preti (ca. 1640)

TEMPTING OFFER?

Since Jesus was human, some people believe the temptations offered by Satan were real. Others say that given Jesus's divine status, he would have been incapable of sin and could not have made a deal with the devil.

▲ *Satan Tempts Jesus in the Desert* by Gustave Doré (1754)

APPROXIMATE TIMELINE

Jesus begins his ministry by being baptized	A.D. 25-26
Jesus fasts and is tempted by Satan	A.D. 25-26

MATTHEW 4, 9; MARK 3; LUKE 5, 6; JOHN 1

Choosing the Disciples

JESUS PICKS 12 MEN WHO WILL
BE WITH HIM FOR THREE YEARS.

As Jesus begins to travel around the countryside preaching, a crowd trails behind eager to hear his message. Like him, they were Jews. Some follow Jesus spontaneously, while others receive personal invitations. Andrew and Peter, for example, are two former disciples of John the Baptist.

ANDREW HEARS (JOHN 1:35-51)

- **Andrew and Peter:** John identifies Jesus as the Messiah and, with another man, begins to heed Jesus's word. Andrew convinces his brother Simon (eventually renamed Peter) to come meet Jesus by telling him,

    "We have found the Messiah."

- **Philip and Nathanael:** In contrast, Jesus reaches out to Philip directly, saying, "Follow me," and Philip does. Philip in turn approaches his friend Nathanael, who is skeptical that anyone from Nazareth could have wisdom worth hearing. He quickly changes his mind once he meets Jesus.

Jesus calls Peter and Andrew to "fish for men" in Duccio di Buoninsegna's *Vocacion De Los Apostoles Pedro Y Andres.* (ca. 1308)

VERSE TO KNOW

"Jesus said to them, 'Follow me and I will make you fish for people.' And immediately they left their nets and followed him." (Mark 1:17, 18)

A STUDENT-TEACHER RELATIONSHIP

Jesus's relationship with his disciples followed Jewish traditions of the era. A rabbi in first-century Judea was a scholar who had spent his life studying Hebrew scriptures to discover how to live to please God. A young man who became a rabbi's disciple would be expected to submit to the rabbi's authority. The rabbi and his disciples would live together and discuss every aspect of their daily lives.

FISHERS OF MEN

Peter, Andrew, James, and John fish all night but come up empty. When Jesus sees them in the morning, he tells them to try again. This time, the catch is so large it starts to rip the nets. Impressed, the four friends quit fishing and accept Jesus's call to become fishers of men.

▲ *The Calling of Saints Peter and Andrew* by Bernardo Strozzi (17th century)

- **Mathew:** Similarly, Jesus issues a personal invitation to Matthew, a tax collector sitting at his tax booth. Seeing potential in the man, Jesus says to him, "Follow me." Matthew gets up, leaves his possessions behind, and begins to follow Jesus.

PRAYING FOR GUIDANCE (MARK 3:13-19; LUKE 6:12-16)

Over time, Jesus gets to know his followers and begins identifying those he wants as his disciples to help spread God's word.

Before Jesus formally identifies his disciples, he spends the night praying for guidance. In the morning, Jesus calls together his large group of followers and from them selects 12 men: Peter, Andrew, James, John, Philip, Bartholomew, Matthew, Thomas, James son of Alphaeus, Simon the Zealot, Judas son of James, and Judas Iscariot.

This group will live with and learn from Jesus over the next three years.

▲ The 12 disciples are represented in the interior of the Church of the Twelve Apostles, a Greek Orthodox church near Caparnuam, Sea of Galilee, Israel.

Jesus (on the left) tells Matthew to become one of his disciples in Van Reymerswaele's *The Calling of St. Matthew.* (16th century)

DO THE DISCIPLES LEAVE THEIR FAMILIES?

After Jesus calls Peter to become his disciple, Peter says, "Look, we have left everything and followed you" (Mark 10:28) implying that he walked away from his family and home to follow Jesus.

However, Mark records that when Jesus leaves the synagogue in Capernaum, he "entered the house of Simon and Andrew" where Peter's mother-in-law was sick in bed. (Mark 1:29)

Whatever was involved in "leaving all" to follow Jesus, Peter still kept his house and family.

———

This fresco from the Basilica of San Giulio, Orta San Giulio, Italy, called *The Four Evangelists*, shows the writers of the four Gospels next to the animals associated with each of them:

- Matthew, a winged angel
- Mark, a winged lion
- Luke, a winged bull
- John, an eagle

One panel of a huge tapestry by Raphael that hangs in the Sistine Chapel. It depicts Jesus's charge to Peter, "Feed my sheep." (ca. 1515)

CHAPTER 9

THE MASTER
TEACHER

Jesus travels from town to town bringing
his lessons to the people. He emphasizes
compassion for others and devotion to the Lord.

A Samaritan does a righteous deed in José Manchola's *The Good Samaritan*. (1852)

This photo, taken of the Inn of the Good Samaritan around 1870, captures the desolation on the road between Jerusalem and Jericho.

MATTHEW 13; LUKE 10

The Parables of Jesus

SIMPLE IN FORM, THESE STORIES ARE PROFOUND IN THEIR MEANING.

When Aesop began telling tales in Greece around 600 B.C., he always provided a moral to explain the lesson. For instance, when a fox turned up his nose at "sour" grapes that he wanted but couldn't reach, the lesson was, "It's easy to despise what you can't get."

But when Jesus shares his stories, called parables, he often leaves the audience to puzzle out their meaning. It is only when he is alone with his disciples that he sometimes explains the tales' deeper meanings.

Jesus tells more than 40 parables, including these most famous ones.

THE GOOD SAMARITAN

When a lawyer asks Jesus, "Who is my neighbor?" Jesus tells the parable of a man traveling from Jerusalem to Jericho who is robbed, beaten, and left for dead. A priest walking by sees him and crosses to the other side of the street. A temple employee also looks but continues on his way. Along comes a Samaritan, a man from population shunned by the Jews. The Samaritan bandages up the man, puts him on his donkey, and takes him to a nearby inn. The Samaritan even leaves money for the innkeeper to take care of the man and promises to come back and check on him.

Jesus then turns the lawyer's question around: "So which of the three was a good neighbor?" He answers, "The one who showed mercy." So Jesus says, "Go and do likewise."

Possible Meaning: Just because you are a "holy" person doesn't mean you are a good person. An outsider who shows compassion is the best neighbor. We are to be good neighbors to those in need.

Fast Forward: Most American states have "Good Samaritan" laws to protect people from being sued when they try to help someone who is injured.

WHO WERE THE SAMARITANS?

Jews who returned from the Babylonian exile found that those who stayed behind in Samaria had abandoned orthodox Judaism and intermarried with local Canaanites. Orthodox Jews not only ostracized the Samaritan Jews, but they also forbade any interaction between the two populations. By the first century A.D., a righteous Jew from Palestine would refuse to even walk through Samaria.

The power of the parable of the Good Samaritan lies in the identity of the hero. To Jesus, doing acts of righteousness can make anyone—even a Samaritan—into a good person.

VERSE TO KNOW

"Then the disciples came and asked him, 'Why do you speak to them in parables?' He answered, 'To you it has been given to know the secrets of the kingdom of heaven, but to them it has not been given.'" (Matthew 13:10-11)

THE PRODIGAL SON

A man has two sons. One day the younger child comes to him and says, "Father, give me the share of the property that will belong to me." When the father does, the youth takes the money, goes far away, and spends it all on wild parties.

When his money is gone, a famine hits the land, and to keep from starving the son finds work taking care of pigs.

One day, when he realizes the pigs' food is starting to look good, the son thinks, *Why don't I go home and throw myself on my father's mercy? Maybe he will employ me.*

As the young man approaches his home, his father comes running and embraces him warmly. The father throws a party for the son, proclaiming, "for this son of mine was dead and is alive again; he was lost and is found!"

Possible Meaning: The father represents God, and the younger son stands for a lost sinner. While God gives people free will and the choice to turn away from him, he is extremely happy when a rebellious child returns.

This parable demonstrates how much God loves and longs to welcome back those who are lost.

▲ Etching of a Bible with Parable of the Prodigal Son by James Tissot (1881)

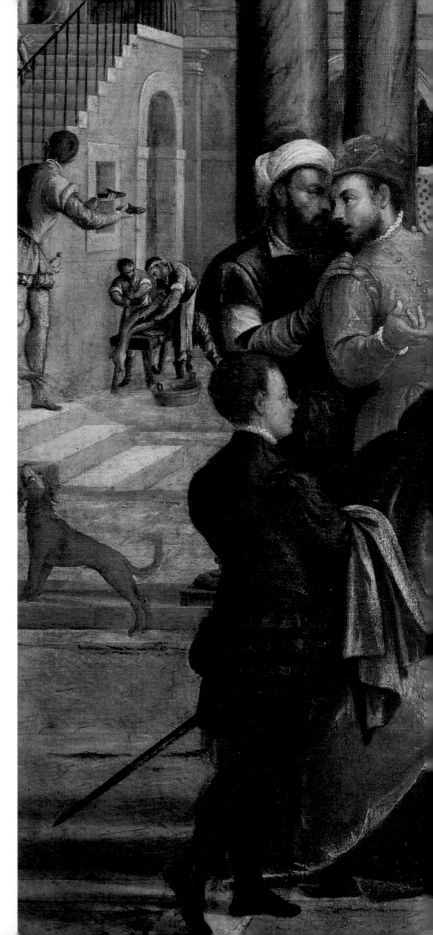

The Prodigal Son by Giovanni Francesco Barbieri, reveals the pathos of the father welcoming home his repentant son. (1618)

Parable of the Lost Sheep from *Brown's Holy Bible* (1754)

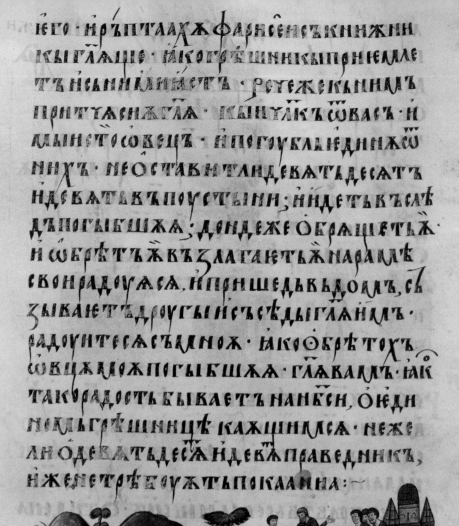

▲ This Bulgarian folio from 1355 depicts the Parable of the Lost Sheep. A good example of late medieval illustrated manuscript, it comes from *The Gospels of Tsar Ivan Alexander*.

THE LOST SHEEP

While talking about how much God values the young, Jesus sets a child on his lap and warns against harming children. Then he tells the story of a shepherd with 100 sheep. When the shepherd counts them and realizes one is missing, he leaves the 99 and goes in search of the missing one. When he finds it, he is happier over that one sheep than the 99 who don't go astray.

Then Jesus hints at his meaning: "It is not the will of your Father in heaven that one of these little ones should be lost."

Possible Meaning: Just as a shepherd is concerned for one sheep that is lost, God cares about each person he has created and his or her eternal fate.

The Sermon on the Mount

THE FIRST TIME JESUS ADDRESSES THE MASSES,
HE DELIVERS UNFORGETTABLE LESSONS.

First-century Jews attending synagogue on the Sabbath are used to hearing teachers expound on the Torah, yet they are unprepared for Jesus's new approach. He does not mimic the scribes' painstaking reference to scripture, but appears to rely on his own authority. Many common people love his fresh approach to Jewish questions, but there are scholars who are disturbed by the implications regarding his identity.

Referred to as the Sermon on the Mount, this discourse contains some of Jesus's most unforgettable teachings.

THE BEATITUDES

Jesus tells people how to be "blessed" or happy, in a way they are unused to. Usually, it is the well off and confident members of the community who receive the blessings; instead, Jesus, harking back to earlier prophets, says the humble, mournful, and meek will attain the Kingdom of Heaven. He even tells his followers to rejoice when they are persecuted because their reward in Heaven will be spectacular.

TURN THE OTHER CHEEK

Jesus expands or reinterprets rules for everything from lust to justice.

- **Murder:** Not only is killing wrong, but individuals should avoid getting so angry with others that they feel provoked to murder.
- **Adultery:** Shunning extramarital sex is not enough. Those who lust after others have already committed adultery in their hearts.
- **Oaths:** Do not swear by Heaven. Let a *yes* be a simple *yes* and a *no* be a simple *no*.
- **Retaliation:** Instead of exacting monetary claims in "an eye for an eye" style of justice, a person who is struck on the cheek should turn the other.
- **Hatred:** People must let go of hatred. They must embrace and pray for their enemies. Then, they will be like God in Heaven.

LEARN SINCERITY

Jesus suggests learning from the mistakes of various Jewish groups. Instead of making a show of one's charity, give to the poor quietly. Rather than praying loudly on street corners, pray in the privacy of one's home. Similarly, when fasting, one should keep his suffering to himself. In this way, followers will be rewarded by God.

JUDGE NOT

A person who judges others will be judged by the same standards. To illustrate, Jesus uses the comical image of a person with a log sticking out of her eye who tries to remove a speck from someone else's.

A RULE THAT IS GOLDEN

Although Judaism taught the lesson of "love thy neighbor as thyself," Jesus restates it: "In everything do to others as you would have them do to you."

▲ Goats climb rocks near the traditional site of the Sermon on the Mount, by an unknown artist.

VERSE TO KNOW
"Now when Jesus had finished saying these things, the crowds were astounded at his teaching, for he taught them as one having authority, and not as their scribes."
(Matthew 7:28-29)

ORIGINAL THOUGHTS
Many of our common sayings come straight from this sermon: *salt of the earth, go the second mile, you can't serve two masters,* and *don't throw pearls before swine.*

Surmon de Jesus-Christ sur la Montagne
by Edouard Dubufe (1844)

VERSE TO KNOW

"Just as you did it to one
of the least of these who
are members of my family,
you did it to me."
(Matthew 25:40)

LUKE 16; MATTHEW 25

Jesus Teaches About Heaven and Hell

DIFFICULT LESSONS ABOUT THE AFTERLIFE

The following two parables suggest
what type of person will be part of
Jesus's kingdom and rewarded at the final
judgment, and what type of person will be
punished and sent to Hades.

RICH VERSUS POOR

While talking to the Pharisees, Jesus
tells the story of Lazarus and the rich
man. The rich man wears fine clothes
and eats sumptuously. Lazarus, a poor

man, covered in sores, comes to his home. The poor man is miserable and longs to eat crumbs from the rich man's table.

But when the men die, things change. The rich man goes to Hades and is tormented, while Lazarus is taken to Abraham's side. The rich man asks for water to cool his tongue. But Abraham tells him there's a chasm between them that prevents anyone from crossing over. The rich man then asks Abraham to send Lazarus to warn his five brothers to change their ways.

Abraham again says no; if the brothers don't already fear God from reading the Scriptures, they won't change no matter who talks to them.

Possible Meaning: The rich man is not punished by God because he is wealthy, but because he is selfish and refuses to help Lazarus.

Those who are rewarded are people who are giving and unselfish.

▲ Teachers of the law argue with Jesus in an attempt to trip him up in James Tissot's *The Pharisees Question Jesus*. (ca. 1886)

▲ A mosaic of the parable of the Good Shepherd detailing the separation of the sheep from the goats from the Basilica of Sant'Apollinare Nuovo, Ravenna, Italy (ca. 6th century)

A FAMILIAR ECHO
Mother Teresa, world famous for caring for the "least of these," said: *"If you can't feed a hundred people, then feed just one."*

THE GOOD SHEPHERD

Jesus tells of a day when the Son of Man returns with his angels and sits on the judgment throne. Gathering the nations before him, Jesus separates them as a shepherd divides sheep and goats: He places the "sheep" at his right hand and the "goats" at his left. Jesus then tells the righteous on his right that because they gave him food, drink, and clothes and were kind to him when he was sick and in prison, they are being rewarded. Wondering, they ask, "When was it that we saw you hungry. . . ?" He tells the nations that when they helped the neediest of those in his family, it was as if they had helped him personally. The righteous go with Jesus into eternal life.

Jesus tells the accursed the opposite: they were never helpful or kind to him.

When this group can't remember any such occasion, Jesus again draws parallels with how this nation treated the needy. The accursed are sent into the eternal punishment.

Possible Meaning: While compassion for strangers is not the only criterion for entering heaven, it is an obvious way to separate those who believe and enter Christ's kingdom and those who don't.

> "Jesus separates them as a shepherd divides sheep and goats . . ." (Matt. 25:32)

Philippe de Champaigne portrays
Jesus in an iconic role in his painting
The Good Shepherd. (ca. 1632)

MARK 2, 14; JOHN 5, 8

Jesus's Teachings Reveal His Identity

IN THE GOSPELS, MANY ARE OFFENDED
BY JESUS'S CLAIMS OF DIVINITY.

Today, even those who are not followers of Jesus accept him as a good man who taught about love. But in many accounts, when Jesus claims divinity, a special relationship to God, or the same powers as God, he is treated as a sinner and a blasphemer. Here are some examples:

THE POWER TO FORGIVE SINS

While Jesus is teaching in Capernaum, four friends bring a lame man to him to be healed. Instead of curing the man, Jesus says, "*Son, your sins are forgiven.*" Jewish leaders, hearing the tale, consider Jesus a blasphemer, as he is claiming the same powers as God. Knowing their thoughts, Jesus asks, "Which is easier, to say to the paralytic, 'Your sins are forgiven,' or to say, 'Stand up and take your mat and walk'?" To show the scholars that he can do both, Jesus proceeds to heal the man.

CALLING HIMSELF THE "SON OF GOD"

While in Jerusalem on the Sabbath, Jesus heals another man who is lame. When the Pharisees accuse Jesus of breaking Sabbath law, he answers, ". . . for whatever the Father does, the Son does likewise." By speaking about God as his Father, Jesus angers the Pharisees who think he is making himself equal to God.

Jesus Healing a Paralytic at Capernaum by an unknown artist

Christ's Discussion with Nicodemus on Eternal Life, a drawing by Julius Schnorr von Carolsfeld (ca. 1830)

THE MAKING OF A MESSIAH

When Jesus is tried before the Jewish council prior to his crucifixion, he is accused of many wrongdoings and gives no response. But when the high priest asks him, "Are you the Messiah, the Son of the Blessed One?" Jesus says, "I am." The high priest, the top official overseeing the Temple, tears his clothes when he hears this answer, for he considers it blasphemous.

HE CLAIMS ETERNAL EXISTENCE

In a discussion with the Jews about Abraham, Jesus states that Abraham was glad to see Jesus's day. When they exclaim, "How could you see Abraham?" Jesus says, "Before Abraham was, I am."

The Jews understand that "I am" is how God identified himself to Moses. (Exodus 3:14) They think Jesus is saying he has always existed and will always exist, just like God.

Jesus preaches to the crowds by the Sea of Galilee, by an unknown artist (ca. 1754)

The Sea of Galilee, Israel

CHAPTER 10

JESUS'S MIRACLES

Through miraculous acts such as giving sight to
the blind, walking on water, and raising the dead,
Jesus supports his claim to be the Son of God.

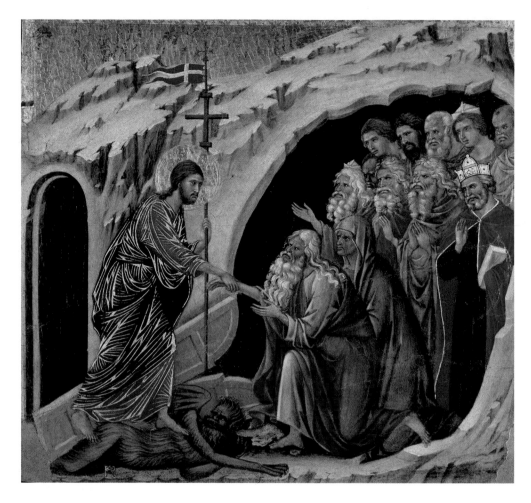

▲ *Maesta (Majesty) Descent Into Limbo* by Duccio di Buoninsegna (mid-13th century)

MATTHEW, MARK, LUKE, JOHN

Curing the Sick and Afflicted

JESUS'S WONDROUS ACTS SHOW HIS POWERS ARE DIVINE AND THAT HE IS THE SON OF GOD.

The English word *miracle* is derived from the Latin "miraculum" and means something that is wondered or marveled at. The miracles recorded in the Gospels do more than cause awe or amazement— they demonstrate divine or supernatural activity at work.

In addition, the miracles define Jesus's identity. He relieves people in severe pain, cures seizures, and reverses paralysis. He gives sight to the blind, heals a shriveled hand, and makes the lame walk. He casts out demons, and brings people back from the dead.

WHY DOES JESUS WORK MIRACLES?
There are several possible reasons why Jesus performs miracles in the

Landscape with Jesus Healing the Blind of Jericho by Philippe de Champaigne (ca. 1640)

Gospels. On the most basic level, the acts are proof that Jesus's powers are divine and thus establish that he is the Son of God.

What's more, Jesus's ability to heal, cast out demons, control the weather, and raise the dead confirms that he is a righteous man sent by God who uses his powers for good and against evil.

The miracles also suggest that Jesus is simply compassionate and good. He heals the sick because he cares about people and wants to help those who are suffering from debilitating diseases.

Finally, when Jesus works miracles, he draws thousands of people to himself, which gives him a platform to teach about the Kingdom of God.

VERSE TO KNOW

"So his fame spread throughout all Syria, and they brought to him all the sick, those who were afflicted with various diseases and pains, demoniacs, epileptics, and paralytics, and he cured them." (Matthew 4:24)

▲ A woman washes in the Pool of Siloam inside the walls of the Old City of Jerusalem where Jesus healed a blind man.

MATTHEW 8, 9; MARK 1, 8; JOHN 9

How Jesus Heals

THE GOSPELS RECORD JESUS PERFORMING MORE THAN 30 DISTINCT MIRACLES.

Jesus uses a variety of methods to heal, depending on the person's needs and level of faith.

- **He cleanses a leper.** Early on, Jesus is approached by a man with leprosy who states, "If you choose, you can make me clean." Jesus reaches out and touches him and then says, "Be made clean!" Immediately, the lesions disappear and the man is made whole again. Jesus then tells the man to show himself to the priest, as required by the law.

- **He opens the eyes of the blind.** In one episode, Jesus is followed by two blind men who cry out for help. Jesus touches the men's eyes and says, "According to your faith let it be done to you," and their eyes are opened.

  Later, asked by a blind man at Bethsaida for aid, Jesus steers the man to a private place and touches his eyes with saliva. Jesus asks the man what he perceives and he replies, "I can see people, but they look like trees, walking." Jesus then lays his hands on

Jesus demonstrates his love for children by allowing this boy to approach him while he is preaching in *Christ and the Little Child*, by an unknown artist. (1897)

DOUBLE VISION: WHY DOES JESUS REQUIRE TWO ATTEMPTS TO HEAL THE MAN AT BETHSAIDA?
This two-part healing may have been Jesus's way of communicating to his disciples that some healing comes gradually.

THE LEPER STIGMA
Just as we quarantine people, animals, and plants to prevent the spread of disease today, Biblical communities also had rules to protect their citizens. In the Old Testament, Leviticus 14 specifically requires a contagious person to appear unkempt, to live apart from others, and to call out "Unclean!" as a warning to fellow citizens.

By the time of the New Testament, infected people are treated as social outcasts and shunned. In touching the leper, Jesus not only crosses strict medical boundaries, he breaks social conventions and makes it possible for the ailing man to re-enter society.

the supplicant's eyes again; after this, the man sees everything clearly.

A man born blind is given a different cure. Spitting on the ground, Jesus makes mud with his saliva and spreads it on the man's eyes. Then he tells him to go wash in the pool of Siloam. The man obeys and comes back seeing.

- **He heals from afar.**
Jesus relays the story of a Roman centurion who asks him to heal his paralyzed servant. When Jesus agrees to travel to the officer's home, the man

> "Jesus then lays his hands on the supplicant's eyes again; after this, the man sees everything clearly."

protests that he is unworthy to have Jesus under his roof. He tells Jesus that to heal the servant, he must simply give the order. "Only speak the word, and my servant will be healed," the man says. "For I also am a man under authority, with soldiers under me; and I say to one, 'Go,' and he goes, and to another, 'Come' and he comes."

Jesus is astonished at the man's great faith and says, "Go; let it be done for you according to your faith." That same hour the centurion's servant is healed.

▲ Jesus's first public miracle happens in Cana where he turns water into wine at a wedding, by an unknown artist. (1754)

———

FAMILIAR PHRASE
Today, saying a person can "walk on water" refers to someone's extraordinary ability to do impossible tasks.

Jesus's Power over Nature, Demons, and Death

HE TURNS WATER INTO WINE, EXORCISES EVIL SPIRITS, AND BRINGS THE DEAD BACK TO LIFE.

———

There are other miracle workers at the time of Jesus; however, none of their wonders compare to his greatest demonstrations of power over nature. Some acts solve mundane problems while others defy weather patterns and sometimes even gravity.

- **He turns water to wine.** Jesus's first natural miracle occurs while he and his mother are guests at a wedding in Cana. Mary alerts him to a problem facing the hosts of the party: They have run out of wine. Mary then tells the attendants, "Do whatever he says." So Jesus has them fill six 30-gallon jars with water and take them to the steward. Once the steward has a sip, he is amazed, as the jars now hold wine of superior quality.

   Without even touching the water, Jesus has turned it into wine.

- **He calms the storm.** The Sea of Galilee can be a dangerous place, especially when a windstorm sweeps down on a small boat that is out on the water. When Jesus and his disciples find themselves in this situation, huge waves rock the boat and fill it with water. While Jesus sleeps soundly, the disciples panic and shake Jesus awake, crying, "Master, we are perishing!" Jesus rebukes the wind with the words, "Peace! Be still!" Immediately, the wind stops and quiet descends, leaving the disciples in a state of awe.

Christ on the Sea of Galilee by an unknown artist (1854)

Matthew is the only disciple who records what happens next. Peter calls out, "Lord, if it is you, command me to come to you on the water." When Jesus says, "Come," Peter crawls out of the boat and starts walking on the water toward Jesus.

Frightened by the waves, Peter begins to sink and cries out, "Lord, save me!" Jesus catches him by the hand and asks the disciple why he doubts. When the men reach the boat, the wind stops. John, in his version of the tale, adds the detail that the boat then immediately reaches the shore.

- **He walks on the waves.** After feeding 5,000 men, women, and children with only five loaves of bread and two fish, Jesus retires to pray. He sends the disciples off in a boat across the Sea of Galilee. Several miles out, they once again find themselves in a terrible storm. Rowing frantically, the disciples see a figure walking toward them in the dim light. Thinking it's a ghost, they cry out in fear. But it is Jesus who speaks to them: "Take heart, it is I; do not be afraid."

- **He puts coins in the mouth of a fish.** One of the more unusual nature miracles occurs when Jesus helps Peter find coins to pay taxes owed the temple authorities.

  Jesus tells Peter to go fishing. He instructs his disciple to throw his hook in the water and to look in the mouth of the first fish that comes up. There, he says, Peter will find a coin that he should use to pay the outstanding tax bill for both Peter and Jesus.

▲ In *Peter Walks on Water*, an unknown artist depicts Peter starting to sink into the water after looking down. (1806)

VERSE TO KNOW

"They were filled with great awe and said to one another, 'Who then is this, that even the wind and the sea obey him?'" (**Mark 4:41**)

▲ The Roman coin Peter finds in the mouth of the fish would have resembled this coin.

Christ the Consoler by Danish artist
Carl Heinrich Bloch (ca. 1870)

Dumb Man Possessed of a Devil by James Tissot (ca. 1875)

DEMONS OBEY JESUS

In Biblical times, it is common for people to complain of being possessed by demons, and some speculate that Satan sends the evil spirits to prevent Jesus from accomplishing his mission.

It is believed that demons are former angels who are urged by Satan to rebel against God and who are cast out of heaven as punishment. The demons then serve Satan and seek to do as much harm as possible to God's kingdom.

One of the worst cases of demon possession that Jesus encounters occurs in Gadarenes country near Galilee. **(Mark 5:2)** As Jesus steps out of the boat, he sees a naked, wild-eyed man trailing broken chains running toward him and screaming.

> "The townspeople . . . are astonished to see the possessed man . . . in his right mind."

Jesus commands the demons to leave the man, but the demons protest saying, "What have you to do with me, Jesus, Son of the Most High God? . . . [D]o not torment me." When Jesus asks the man his name, he replies, "My name is Legion, for we are many."

The demons ask for permission to enter a nearby herd of pigs, and Jesus agrees. When the spirits inhabit the bodies of the swine, the animals rush down into the lake and drown themselves.

As the townspeople come out, they are astonished to see the possessed man clothed and in his right mind. Though the man asks to join Jesus on his voyage, Jesus instructs him to return home and tell others how much God has done for him.

A DISCREPANCY

Mark, Luke, and Matthew all recount the exorcism at Gadarenes, but Matthew describes two demoniacs, while Mark and Luke have one. Why the discrepancy? It is possible two possessed people were present, but Mark and Luke focused on the one who was most notorious and disturbed.

DEMONIAC MOTIVES

(1) They understand who Jesus is and are afraid of him. (2) They don't want to go to a place of torment before they have to. (3) They cause destruction in any living being they enter.

WHAT'S IN A NAME?

The demon in the story in Mark 5 who identifies himself as "Legion," or many, comes from the region of Gadarenes, which means mass defection.

Ne vo laisse vaincre du mal S maf vaing le mal y le bn Ro·3· car ni est la coqe se leiue. Tout arbre qi ne porte bon fruit sera coupe et recte au feu Mat·3·

vous vue selon la chair vous mourez Rom·8·13

Coupe le auin bien ne fart y qu accuper la terre luc·13·7·

Seigneur laisse le encore cette annee luce·13·8· parce donne parce populo tuo

Arbres fletrisfans fans fruicts deus fois morts & derathines ausquel est appreshee lobsurite des tenebres eternellement Jude·13·C·13

▲ Jesus rings a bell while the skeleton hacks off tree limbs in the allegorical *The Tree of Good and Evil* by an unknown artist. (16th century)

THE DISCIPLES NEED HELP (MARK 9:14-28)

While Jesus is away traveling, a man brings his mute, epileptic, and demon-possessed son to the disciples. Although the disciples have cast out demons before, they are unable to help the boy and the man waits for Jesus's returns.

Seeing Jesus, the man runs and begs for assistance. He tells the story of a spirit who throws the boy into the fire or into water to try to kill him. Jesus then speaks to the demon and commands it to come out of the boy's body. The spirit causes a great convulsion as it leaves, and the boy lies like a corpse. But Jesus takes him by the hand and lifts him up, and he is completely healed.

On the surface, this seems like another simple miracle story. However, it focuses even more explicitly on faith. When the desperate father, at his wits' end, asks for Jesus's healing, he is still afraid that his son is beyond help. Jesus's answer is meant not just for

the father to hear, but for the disciples, the gathering crowd, and modern-day readers too. Jesus said to him, "If you are able!—All things can be done for the one who believes." Immediately the father of the child cried out, "I believe; help my unbelief!"

Those five words reveal much about the change in the father. He is no longer waiting on Jesus to use his power to cure his son. Jesus is waiting on him to stop suffering through a lack of faith. The father is able to feel the power of belief, belief that his child's possession is weaker than Jesus's power. The father is beginning to understand that his unbelief is causing the suffering. By asking for help, he is letting Jesus know he understands that nothing is more powerful than belief without doubt. Many believe the true moral of this story is that suffering comes not from a lack of faith, but from a struggle for a faith without doubts.

▲ The Italian artist known as Veronese depicts Jesus raising a boy from the dead in *The Awakening of the Young Man of Nain*. (1565–1570)

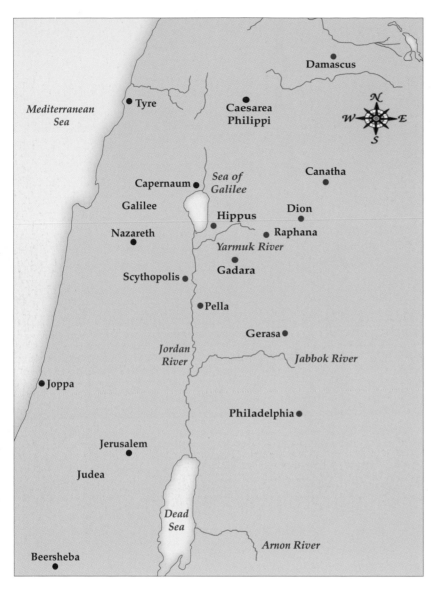

◀ Jesus spent much of his time ministering in the region called the Decapolis, 10 mostly Roman cities (marked in red) east of the Sea of Galilee.

sisters, Martha and Mary, and often stays in their home in Bethany near Jerusalem. When Lazarus becomes very sick, the sisters send word to Jesus.

JESUS ARRIVES ON HIS OWN TIME

Jesus doesn't respond right away. Rather than hurrying to Lazarus's side, he remains where he is for two days, telling his disciples, "This illness does not lead to death; rather it is for God's glory, so that the Son of God may be glorified through it." When Jesus is ready to leave on the journey to Bethany, he tells his followers, "Our friend Lazarus has fallen asleep, but I am going there to awaken him."

By the time Jesus reaches Bethany, Lazarus has been dead for four days. First Martha and then Mary go out to talk to him. Each is overcome with grief and can't understand why Jesus didn't arrive earlier to save their brother. When he sees their grief, he weeps also.

LAZARUS, COME OUT!

The sisters and the crowd of mourners all go with Jesus and the disciples to Lazarus's tomb in a nearby cave. Jesus startles them by ordering, "Take away the stone." Martha protests saying, "Lord, already there is a stench because he has been dead four days." Jesus counsels her, "Did I not tell you that if you believed, you would see the glory of God?" Jesus prays, thanking the Father for always hearing him. He cries with a loud voice, "Lazarus, come out!"

Then Lazarus walks out, bound in his burial clothes, and Jesus tells the mourners, "Unbind him, and let him go."

UNBIND HIM!

Jesus gives the command to unbind Lazarus because, according to Jewish burial customs, he would have been wrapped from head to foot in linen cloth.

_____

DEATH WISHES

Why wait until Lazarus is dead for four days? Jews at the time believed that a soul stayed near the grave three days hoping to return to the body. After four days, there was no hope.

DEATH IS DEFEATED

While the Gospels tell of two other occasions when Jesus raises someone from the dead—the widow of Nain's only son and Jairus's daughter—the account of Jesus raising Lazarus is the most detailed and dramatic.

It is also the final act that inspires Jesus's enemies to begin actively seeking his death.

Jesus is good friends with Lazarus and his two

"Rather than hurrying to Lazarus's side, he remains where he is for two days, telling his disciples, 'This illness does not lead to death . . .'"

The Resurrection of Lazarus by
Jean-Baptiste Corneille (ca. 1680)

▲ Jesus spends the week before his crucifixion in the village of Bethany, the home of Mary, Martha, and Lazarus, by an unknown artist. (ca. 1754)

UNITED AGAINST JESUS

Many observers present at Lazarus's resurrection spread the word, but loyalties are divided. Some people go straight to Mary. Others report to the Pharisees, the legal religious group that follows the Old Testament, believes in the ministry of angels, and supports the concept of an afterlife.

Worried by Jesus's miracles, apparent claims, and increasingly popular ministry, the Pharisees decide to consult a rival religious group, the Sanhedrin, whose high priests accept only the writings of Moses and deny the resurrection of souls. The two groups agree to put aside their religious differences and to convene a council to discuss the events at Bethany.

Initially, the council focuses on the Romans, who members say are threatened by Jesus's growing number of followers.

They worry that "If we let him go on like this," the Romans will come and destroy the temple and the entire Jewish nation in order to stamp out Jesus's influence.

A PROPOSAL FROM A HIGH PRIEST

Rather than risk the fate of all Jews, Caiaphas, the Sanhedrin high priest, says it would be better that Jesus "should die for the people." His proposal reflects the Jewish view of corporality, where one person, good or bad, can affect the fate of the whole community. As high priest, Caiaphas prophesized that Jesus will die for the nation and for the benefit of all Jews. The council agrees Jesus should be put to death.

Jesus withdraws from the Jewish community and goes to a town called Ephraim to be with his disciples.

Jesus thus sets in motion mechanisms that will lead to his crucifixion.

▲ *Jesus Feeding the Multitude, The Miracle of Loaves and Fishes*, a chromolithograph by J.M. Kronheim (1869)

CHAPTER 11

JESUS'S DEATH, BURIAL, AND RESURRECTION

Often referred to as the Passion, the trials and execution of Jesus make for compelling reading. There's political intrigue, betrayal by a trusted companion, and true pathos. The events form the basis for much of Christian theology, including the key concepts of atonement and salvation.

Crucifixion with God the Father and Saint Ignatius of Loyola by Francesco Fontebasso (18th century)

Entry Of Christ Into Jerusalem
by Charles Le Brun (1659)

Dramatic Entry into Jerusalem

JESUS RIDES INTO THE CITY OF DAVID ON A HUMBLE DONKEY.

A RIGHTFUL HEIR TO DAVID'S THRONE
By making the kind of triumphal entry usually afforded rulers and generals, Jesus is declaring that he comes to the city as a ruler, the rightful heir to David's throne. He also fulfills Zechariah's prophecy that the Messiah would enter Jerusalem on a colt. The people celebrate Jesus's arrival, but they will soon be disappointed to realize his reign is not about conquering Rome but about ushering in the Kingdom of God.

Many biographers devote little space to the deaths of their subjects, yet the writer of each Gospel spends more than a quarter of his story relating events surrounding the killing of Jesus. Clearly, the crucifixion and what follows are of central importance to the story of Christianity.

HIGH HOPES AND EVIL PLOTS
People from the countryside flood into Jerusalem to celebrate Passover and to see Jesus. Tensions run high in the city because they expect a confrontation between Jesus and the Jewish authorities.

When some followers of Jesus report to Caiaphas, the high priest, that Jesus raised Lazarus from the dead, Caiaphas and the Jewish authorities decide that Jesus must die. They plan to seize him when he arrives in Jerusalem for Passover. Jesus, knowing of their plans, decides to stay away from Jerusalem and instead, quietly settles in the village of Bethany with his disciples for Passover week.

In Jerusalem, the Pharisees announce that anyone who sees Jesus must report it so he can be captured. The people speculate whether Jesus is truly the Messiah. Many wonder whether Jesus will overthrow the Romans.

JESUS ORGANIZES A PARADE

On the Sunday morning before Passover, Jesus plans events so he can enter Jerusalem in a dramatic way. He sends two disciples into the village to find a donkey and her colt and to bring them back to him. When bystanders ask the men what they are doing, they simply say, "The Lord needs it," and they let it go. After the disciples put robes on the colt, Jesus mounts it and heads into Jerusalem.

The Passover crowds see him coming and happily join the procession, throwing their garments in front of him and waving palm branches. Jesus's entry into Jerusalem is a triumph.

▲ The words *House of David* are inscribed on this stone, which was uncovered at Tel Dan in Israel.

▲ Marco d'Oggiono's *The Last Supper* is a copy from the 16th century of Leonardo da Vinci's masterpiece.

TABLE MANNERS
Unlike the scene shown above in this copy of da Vinci's *The Last Supper*, 1st-century diners reclined on couches, propped on an elbow, with their feet out behind them. The position would make it easy for Jesus to move around and wash each person's feet.

MATTHEW 26; MARK 14; LUKE 22; JOHN 13

A Dinner to Remember

JESUS CHOOSES AN INTIMATE SETTING TO SHARE HIS LAST MEAL WITH HIS DISCIPLES.

Though Jesus foresees the suffering he is about to endure, he no longer is focused on the Pharisees or the Sanhedrin who have for so long challenged his ministry and persecuted him. Instead, he uses his final meal to prepare his disciples for what is about to happen.

THE LAST SUPPER
To ensure privacy, Jesus gives Peter and John cryptic

VERSE TO KNOW
"Jesus knew that his hour had come to depart from this world and go to the Father."
(John 13:1)

instructions for finding a place to share the Passover meal. They are to follow a man carrying a pitcher of water into a house and ask the owner to allow them to meet in his upper room. Then, with help from the man's family, the disciples are to collect the necessary ingredients for the feast: a roasted lamb, unleavened bread, wine, bitter herbs, and other symbolic items.

When evening arrives, the disciples settle themselves around the table for the seder. Silently, Jesus rises and wraps a towel around himself, gets a basin of water, and begins washing the disciples' feet.

He announces as they eat that one of the gathered will betray him. Judas, who secretly has agreed with the leaders of the Jewish community to reveal Jesus's whereabouts in exchange for 30 pieces of silver, is taken aback and cries out, "Surely

In *Last Supper*, Paolo Caliari paints Jesus blesses an apostle. (16th century)

not I, Rabbi?" Jesus responds "You have said so."

As Judas departs, Jesus further alarms his followers by telling them they will all abandon him when he is in danger. Peter vehemently protests that he will never leave Jesus and is deeply grieved when Jesus predicts Peter will deny him three times.

Using two elements of the Passover meal, Jesus first picks up the unleavened bread, gives thanks, breaks it into pieces, and hands a bit to each disciple. Then he says, "This is my body, which is given for you. Do this in remembrance of me." He then takes a cup of wine, gives thanks, and passes the vessel around for all to drink saying, "This cup that is poured out for you is the new covenant in my blood."

Thus Jesus institutes the Eucharist sacrament most Christian denominations follow today.

> "This is my body, which is given for you." (Luke 22:19)

WHAT IS THE EUCHARIST? What do the bread and wine stand for? Jesus wants to establish a ritual by which his followers will remember his death. By eating broken pieces of bread, they will think about his crucified body; by drinking wine, they will be reminded of his blood shed for them. To this day, Christians around the world repeat this rite in what is known as "Communion," "The Lord's Supper," or the "Eucharist."

MATTHEW 26, 27; MARK 14, 15; LUKE 22

Jesus Prays in the Garden

TROUBLE FOLLOWS A QUIET MOMENT
OF PRAYER IN A GARDEN.

After the Passover meal, Jesus leads his disciples to the Garden of Gethsemane, where most of the men fall asleep. He walks deeper into the brush with Peter, James, and John and asks them to stay awake, watch, and pray. Jesus moves to be by himself and addresses God while Peter, James, and John sleep briefly. Their night is about to unravel in a series of terrifying events.

PRAYER IN THE GARDEN

In deep anguish, Jesus throws himself to the ground and prays to the Lord. Three times he begs his Father to find a way to spare his life and prevent him from being crucified for the sins of the world. Jesus's pain is so great that "his sweat became like great drops of blood falling down on the ground" but each prayer concludes with, "Yet not what I want, but what you want." After the third request, Jesus accepts his fate and goes to awaken his sleeping disciples.

In *The Prayer in the Garden of Olives*, an unknown artist portrays an angel ministering to Jesus.

The Kiss of Judas by Giotto, detail from the cycle of frescoes *Life and Passion of Christ* (1303–1305) in Scrovegni Chapel, Padua, Italy

MATTHEW 27; MARK 14, 15; JOHN 18

Jesus Is Betrayed and Arrested

BEFORE HE IS CRUCIFIED, JESUS IS PUT ON TRIAL SEVEN TIMES.

Suddenly the dark night lights up with torches as Judas leads a crowd of armed guards into the garden. To identify Jesus, Judas goes up and kisses him. When the guards move in, Peter draws a sword and cuts off one man's ear. But Jesus tells him to put his sword away. He then heals the man's ear and submits as they tie him up and lead him to prison.

ACCUSED OF BLASPHEMY

The guards bring Jesus to Caiaphas, who assembles the Jewish council for a hasty trial. False witnesses are produced but not needed as Jesus gives the council the proof they need to convict him when he states that he is the Messiah. Caiaphas declares Jesus guilty of blasphemy, and the council pronounces his death sentence. After he is beaten, they take him to Pontius Pilate, the Roman governor.

Pilate listens to the Jewish leaders' accusations against Jesus, but is uninterested in their charge of blasphemy. Instead, he

Christ Before Pontius Pilate by an unknown artist

focuses on one claim and asks Jesus, "Are you the King of the Jews?" When Jesus says he is and that his kingdom is not of this world, Pilate seems reluctant to pronounce a death sentence and tries several maneuvers:

- First, he sends Jesus to Herod, who has jurisdiction over Galileans. Jesus, however, refuses to speak to Herod or perform any miracles, and Herod returns him to Pilate.

- The Roman governor then tries to convince the Jews that he should only punish Jesus, not kill him. Pilate has Jesus flogged, clothed in a royal robe and a crown of thorns, and brought out for the Jewish elders to see. But instead of feeling pity for Jesus, the crowd shouts "Crucify him!"

- Finally, as part of the Roman custom of releasing a prisoner on Passover, Pilate offers the crowd the choice of freeing Barabbas, a murderer, or Jesus. Prompted by the Jewish leaders, they call out, "Not this man, but Barabbas!" When Pilate says, "Here is the man!" the crowd chants, "Crucify him!" Fearing a riot, Pilate condemns Jesus to death. But first he publicly washes his hands, stating, "I am innocent of this man's blood."

▲ This path runs through olive trees in the Garden of Gethsemane where Jesus prayed with his disciples the night he was arrested.

ON PAIN OF DEATH
Roman floggings were especially cruel. After a prisoner was stripped and tied to a post, he was beaten with a leather whip that had thongs tied with shards of bone and lead balls.

The Descent from the Cross is the central panel of the triptych by an unknown artist.

MATTHEW 27; MARK 15; LUKE 23; JOHN 19
Buried in a Cave
A FOLLOWER EMERGES TO PROVIDE
A TOMB FOR THE BODY OF JESUS.

Under Roman law, criminals executed for sedition are usually denied the dignity of burial and left on the cross to be eaten by vultures. Jews in contrast, bury executed criminals, but not in family plots, to avoid desecrating the dead.

Following the crucifixion, Joseph of Arimathea, a believer, comes forward and asks to take possession of the body. He wants to give Jesus a proper burial before the Sabbath, even if it puts his own reputation and safety at risk. For Joseph, faith outweighs any consequences that may follow.

With the help of Nicodemus, a Pharisee who favored Jesus, Joseph wraps the body of Jesus in linen along with spices, places it in his own family's plot in a cave, and rolls a large stone in front to seal the tomb.

By overseeing the burial of the accused Jesus, Joseph of Arimathea is demonstrating his faith to his family, his friends, and the public. He puts his reputation on the line to provide Jesus a proper burial.

▲ Willem Key portrays Mary, Jesus's mother, after he is taken off the cross in *Mourning of Christ*. (ca. 1545)

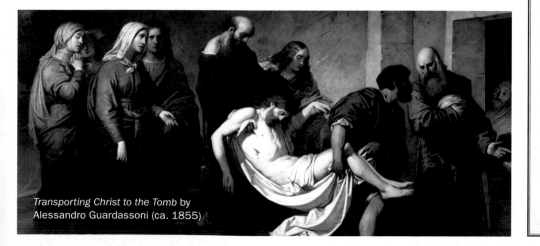

Transporting Christ to the Tomb by Alessandro Guardassoni (ca. 1855)

FINAL WORDS

JESUS SPEAKS ONLY SEVEN TIMES DURING HIS SIX HOURS ON THE CROSS.

1. "Father, forgive them; for they do not know what they are doing." (Luke 23:34) As the soldiers who nail him to the cross begin to mock him, Jesus asks God to forgive them.

2. "Truly I tell you, today you will be with me in Paradise." (Luke 23:43) Hanging between two criminals being crucified, Jesus responds to one's request to remember him.

3. "Woman, here is your son." Then he said to the disciple, "Here is your mother." (John 19:26-27) Seeing his grieving mother standing nearby, Jesus asks John to take care of her.

4. "My God, my God, why have you forsaken me?" (Matthew 27:46) Jesus cries this out in the final hour of his life as he bears the sins of the world and feels deserted by God.

5. "I am thirsty." (John 19:28) Jesus says the only expression related to physical suffering at the very end.

6. "Father, into your hands I commend my spirit." (Luke 23:46) Jesus cries out in a loud voice, and he dies.

7. "It is finished." (John 19:30) Jesus says this at the moment of his death, knowing that his mission on Earth had been accomplished.

▲ *Ecce Homo* (Behold the Man) by Andrea Solario (16th century)

MATTHEW 28; MARK 16; LUKE 24; JOHN 20

Jesus Rises from the Grave

MARY MAGDALENE FINDS HIS TOMB EMPTY.

Friday evening and Saturday, Jesus's friends and enemies consider the meaning of his death and burial. But on Sunday, all understanding is overturned as an earthquake rattles the land and an angel descends from Heaven like a streak of lightning. As told in Matthew, the angel rolls the stone from Jesus's tomb, so frightening the armed guards posted outside that they swoon and faint. When the soldiers revive, they find the tomb empty, rush to tell the Jewish leaders, and are bribed to say Jesus's disciples stole the body.

As this scene unfolds, Mary makes her way to the tomb with a group of women to bring more spices. Seeing the disarray Mary Magdalene runs to tell Peter and John that Jesus's body is missing. According to Mark, the other women are told by an angel that Jesus has risen from the dead. They are commanded to go and spread the word to the disciples.

John writes that he and Peter race to the tomb to confirm Mary Magdalene's report. The disciples are both startled to see the burial clothes lying in place.

JESUS APPEARS TO MARY

John and Peter depart to find the other disciples, while Mary Magdalene lingers outside the tomb weeping. When she sees a man she assumes to be the gardener, she asks him whether he knows where Jesus's body is. She hears the man say, "Mary!" and she immediately knows it is Jesus. As she clings to him, Jesus tells her to spread the word to his disciples. Soon after this encounter, Jesus also appears to the other women on their return journey and repeats his message to spread the word.

The disciples, however, are skeptical, according to Luke, and don't believe it when the women say they've seen Jesus alive. Returning from the cave, Peter joins the disciples and says the Lord has also appeared to him. Later that night, the disciples except for Thomas gather in a locked room. Two men come and tell of meeting, talking, and eating with Jesus that afternoon.

Jesus appears in the room and says, "Peace be with you." At first the disciples think Jesus is a ghost, but he encourages them to touch his hands, feet, and side. He eats a piece of broiled fish to further convince them. Finally, the men believe that Jesus has, in fact, risen from the dead.

The Resurrection by
Dutch painter Adriaen
van der Werff (ca. 1690)

Ascension De Cristo Ante Los Discipulos by an unknown artist

MATTHEW 28; LUKE 24; JOHN 20, 21; ACTS 1

Ascending to Heaven

THE GOSPELS RECORD JESUS
RISING BODILY INTO THE SKY.

▲ *Delivery of the Keys to St. Peter* by Jean Auguste Dominique Ingres (ca. 1810)

In the 40 days following his resurrection, Jesus appears to the disciples several times to show that he is alive and to prepare them for his eventual departure.

OTHER RESURRECTION APPEARANCES

Since Thomas was not present on resurrection Sunday, he refuses to believe until he sees and touches Jesus himself. A week later, when Jesus appears to the disciples the second time, he invites Thomas to touch his side. Thomas gazes at him in awe and declares, "My Lord and my God!"

Jesus arranges to meet his disciples in Galilee. There are seven present, including Peter, James, and John, and they are fishing. When they catch nothing, someone on the shore instructs them to cast their nets on the right side of the boat to fill their nets. John looks more closely at the man and exclaims, "It is the Lord!" Peter jumps in and swims to shore.

"DO YOU LOVE ME?"

Jesus has lit a fire and invites the disciples to cook some of the fish on it. While they eat, Jesus turns to Peter and asks him three times, "Do you love me?" Each time, Peter replies that he does, and Jesus tells him, "Feed my sheep."

FINAL INSTRUCTIONS

While the disciples are still in Galilee, Jesus appears to them on a mountain, and they worship him. Then he gives them what is known as the Great Commission: "Go therefore and make disciples of all nations, baptizing them in the name of the Father and of the Son and of the Holy Spirit, and teaching them to obey everything that I have commanded you. And remember, I am with you always, to the end of the age." **(Matthew 28:19, 20)**

When the disciples return to Jerusalem, Jesus tells them to stay there until they receive power from the Holy Spirit so they will be able to be his witnesses to the ends of the Earth. As they watch, Jesus is lifted up, and a cloud takes him out of their sight. Two angels appear and tell them some day Jesus will return in the same way.

> **VERSE TO KNOW**
> "Do not be afraid; go and tell my brothers to go to Galilee; there they will see me."
> **(Matthew 28:10)**

WHAT IS A DOUBTING THOMAS?

We refer to someone as a "Doubting Thomas" when he or she is skeptical and refuses to believe things without a high standard of proof.

GREAT COMMISSION VERUS THE LIMITED COMMISSION

Jesus gives two commissions to his disciples. The Great Commission, cited in the text to the left, is delivered after Jesus spends three years with his disciples and after his resurrection. In it, Jesus tells his disciples to go to all the nations of the world.

The limited commission, from Matthew 10, happens during the three years Jesus is training his disciples. He wants to limit who the disciples talk to, so he tells them just go to the "lost sheep of the house of Israel." **(Matthew 10:6)**

The Death Of Sapphira
by Nicolas Poussin (1652)

CHAPTER 12

THE ACTS OF THE APOSTLES

Acts, the fifth book in the New Testament, records the history of the early Church after Jesus's death and chronicles how his message spreads beyond the Jewish community and into the Gentile world, where it quickly takes hold.

Who Was Luke?

WRITER, PHYSICIAN, AND HISTORIAN
OF THE EARLY CHURCH

WHO WROTE ACTS?

Many people believe that Luke wrote Acts of the Apostles and the Gospel that bears his name—even though the writer of both works chose to remain anonymous. The assumption is based on a number of factors. For one, it is widely believed that Luke was a traveling companion to Paul and some passages in Acts are written in the first person plural, or "we" instead of "they"—suggesting that the author was an eyewitness to the events described. What's more, the author of the Gospel of Luke refers to it as his "first book." Lastly, Acts and Luke both are dedicated to a man named Theophilus.

WHAT DO WE KNOW ABOUT LUKE?

Although the New Testament does not give a lot of background information about Luke, scholars agree that he was well educated.

- **Physician:** Luke is believed to have been a doctor. In Colossians 4:14, Paul refers to him as "Luke, the beloved physician." Other words Luke uses in his Gospel and Acts also suggest a medical background.
- **Writer:** Luke's education can also be seen by his use of sophisticated Greek. The way Luke wrote—his extensive vocabulary and ability to write in a variety of literary styles—reveals a man trained in rhetoric.
- **Companion:** Acts 16 records its narrator with Paul and Silas at Troas during his second missionary journey. When Paul sends greetings from his companions to the Church in Colossae in Asia Minor, he includes Luke's name.

▲ *St Luke with the Virgin and St Paul* by Muzio Sforza (ca. 1490)

THE FACTS OF ACTS

Acts includes specific references to a wide variety of people, government officials, and court proceedings in particular places. Acts 17, for example, refers to "politarchs" in Thessalonica. Modern archaeology has unearthed inscriptions that confirm the use of this regional title in Macedonia. Another example is the many references in Acts 24–26 to Felix and Festus as "Procurators of Judea." Nonbiblical sources such as bronze Roman coins minted by Festus confirm the existence of these men, their titles, and the cities where they both try Paul in court.

Juan Bautista Maíno shows the Holy Spirit descending on Mary and the disciples in *The Pentecost.* (ca. 1611)

ACTS 1, 2

Peter Preaches on Pentecost

THE FISHERMAN OF GALILEE GIVES
AN IMPASSIONED SPEECH.

The Day of Pentecost changes everything for the followers of Jesus. They find new courage to preach, teach, and heal in the name of the Son.

A NEW PETER

As leader of the disciples, Peter is often unstable and impulsive. He collapses when Jesus is arrested and vehemently denies even knowing him. But when Peter sees Jesus alive after his death and knows he has been forgiven for his failures, he changes. He becomes a new kind of leader with a unique combination of humility and boldness.

The real turning point for Peter comes on the Day of Pentecost, 50 days after Jesus's death. According to Jesus's instructions, the disciples are waiting in Jerusalem for the promised gift of baptism from the Holy Spirit. Ten days after Jesus's return to Heaven, they are praying together with 120 other believers when the sound of a violent wind fills the house. Suddenly, what looks like tongues of fire come to rest on the disciples. Filled with the Holy Spirit, they begin to speak in foreign languages they have never learned.

Jews from around the civilized world have gathered in Jerusalem to celebrate the Day of the Pentecost. When the crowd hears the sound of the wind, they gather around the disciples and are astonished to hear them speaking in their own languages. But some mock them and say they are drunk.

Peter stands up and says, "Indeed, these are not drunk, as you suppose, for it is only nine o'clock in the morning. No, this is what was spoken through the prophet Joel:

'In the last days it will be, God declares, that I will pour out my Spirit upon all flesh, and your sons and your daughters shall prophesy.' " **(Acts 2:15)**

Peter delivers the first Gospel message, telling the crowd that Jesus was sent by God and performed many miracles. He continues, saying that Jesus was put to death on the cross with the help of wicked men, but was raised from the dead by God "and of that all of us are witnesses." **(Acts 2:32)**

Peter references the Old Testament prophecies to make a point about those who are guilty of crucifying Jesus. When the crowd hears this, they are horrified and call out, "Brothers, what should we do?" Peter tells them to repent and be baptized in the name of Jesus. If they do, their sins will be forgiven and God's Holy Spirit will come to live inside them. Many of them believe, and 3,000 are baptized that day. And with that act, the Christian Church begins.

VERSE TO KNOW

"Peter said to them, 'Repent, and be baptized every one of you in the name of Jesus Christ so that your sins may be forgiven; and you will receive the gift of the Holy Spirit.'" (Acts 2:38)

WHAT IS MEANT BY A "GOSPEL MESSAGE"?
The word "gospel" means Good News. So anyone who tells the story of Jesus's death, burial, and resurrection and invites people to put their faith in him as the Son of God is preaching the Gospel.

WHEN WERE FOLLOWERS OF JESUS FIRST CALLED CHRISTIANS?
Followers of Christ were not always called Christians. At first, they were simply called "followers of the Way." In Acts 9, Saul (Paul) asks the Jewish leaders in Jerusalem for permission to persecute the followers of "the Way," or believers in Jesus. However, this changes. In Acts 11, followers of the Way are called Christians for the first time. "So it was that for an entire year they met with the Church, and taught a great many people and it was in Antioch that the disciples were first called Christians" (Acts 11:26)

WHAT WAS THE DAY OF PENTECOST?
Judaism and Christianity both have a spring holiday tied to the Greek word for 50th day, or Pentecost. In Judaism, the feast is known as Shavuot and commemorates 50 days after Passover. In Christianity, the festival is called Pentecost and marks the 50-day period following Easter Sunday.

Saint Peter Healing the Cripple by Simone Cantarini known as il Pesarese (17th century)

ACTS 4–5
Peter Performs Miracles and Gets Arrested

PETER AND THE FOLLOWERS OF THE WAY SUFFER FOR PREACHING AND HEALING.

Because of their determination to preach about Jesus wherever they go, Peter and the other apostles keep angering the authorities. Each time, the penalty worsens, until finally James is martyred in a beheading, and Peter's life is endangered.

HEALING A CRIPPLED BEGGAR
A man lame from birth is being carried into the temple in Jerusalem to beg when he spots Peter and John and asks them for money. Peter says he doesn't have any but he'll give him something better. He declares: "In the name of Jesus Christ of Nazareth, stand up and walk." Suddenly, the man not only walks, he begins leaping around and praising God. When the crowd sees who has been healed, they are amazed and begin to gather around Peter and John.

Peter then tells the people it's in the name of Jesus the man was healed. He reminds them that Jesus was crucified, but God raised him up. While he and John are still speaking, the Jewish leaders come up and are angered to hear them preaching about Jesus. They are arrested and taken to custody.

The next day, the high priest and other Jewish leaders question Peter and John. The leaders threaten them, and tell them to stop talking about Jesus. But they reply, "Whether it is right in God's sight to listen to you rather than to God, you must judge; for we cannot keep from speaking about what we have seen and heard." **(Acts 4:19–20)**

PERFORMING MORE MIRACLES
The men are released by an angel, who tells them to keep preaching. When the high priest sends for the disciples, he is informed by temple police that Peter and John have escaped and are preaching again.

> **VERSE TO KNOW**
> "But Peter and the apostles answered, "We must obey God rather than any human authority." **(Acts 5:29)**

Giovanni Francesco Guerrieri paints the angel freeing Peter in *St Peter in Prison*. (1610–1620)

Frustrated, the high priest has the men brought back in and exclaims, "We gave you strict orders not to preach in this name." But Peter and the others say they must obey God, not man. So the high priest has them beaten and then releases them. The apostles leave rejoicing that they have been allowed to suffer for Jesus's sake.

THE BELIEVERS SHARE THEIR POSSESSIONS

Luke reports that the group of believers decides to voluntarily sell all they possess, pool their money, and live off a common fund. Some followers sell their possessions including land and houses and give that money to the apostles who distribute it to whomever is in need.

ANANIAS AND SAPPHIRA

Acts 5 records the troubling story of how Ananias and his wife, Sapphira, also sell some land they own. But instead of voluntarily donating all the money to the common pool, they keep some of it and pretend they have donated the whole amount. When Ananias stands before Peter to make the donation, Peter says, "Why has Satan filled your heart to lie to the Holy Spirit and to keep back part of the proceeds of the land? ... You did not lie to us but to God!" **(Act 5:3-4)** Then Ananias falls to the ground dead.

Sapphira shows up three hours later unaware of what happened to Ananias. When Peter confronts her with the truth, she too collapses and dies.

Roman ruins of a temple in Caesarea, Israel. Peter may have passed through this temple when the Spirit sends him to meet Cornelius.

WHAT IS A GENTILE?

A Gentile is a person of non-Jewish heritage. Sometimes the Jews referred to Gentiles as "the uncircumcised."

VERSE TO KNOW

"For in the one Spirit we were all baptized into one body—Jews or Greeks, slaves or free—and we were all made to drink of one Spirit."
(1 Corinthians 12:13)

ACTS 10

Peter and the First Gentile Convert

THE EARLIEST FOLLOWERS OF JESUS WERE JEWS. THEN PETER MEETS CORNELIUS.

God carefully choreographs a meeting between two men from very different backgrounds. The encounter, between Peter and Cornelius, a Roman centurion, will change the course of Christianity as Cornelius becomes the first Gentile, or non-Jewish follower, of Jesus.

- **Day 1, Caesarea, 3:00 p.m.**
Cornelius is a very devout man who gives generously to the poor and prays constantly to the God of Israel. One afternoon he is visited by an angel who tells him, "Your prayers and your alms have ascended as a memorial before God. Now send men to Joppa for a certain Simon who is called Peter." Cornelius calls in three trusted men, tells them everything, and sends them to Joppa.

- **Day 2, Joppa, Noon**
Peter is up on the roof praying when he gets hungry. Falling into a trance, he sees Heaven open and a large sheet being lowered full of animals, reptiles, and birds. A voice tells him, "Get up, Peter; kill and eat." But since there are unclean animals in the sheet, Peter protests: "By no means, Lord; for I have never eaten anything that is profane or unclean." The voice replies, "What God has made clean,

you must not call profane." This happens three times, and the sheet returns to Heaven. While Peter is puzzling over the meaning of his vision, the Spirit tells him, "Look, three men are searching for you. Now get up, go down, and go with them without hesitation, for I have sent them." Cornelius's three men arrive just then, and Peter invites them in to be his guests.

- **Day 3, From Joppa to Caesarea**
The next day Peter sets out with the three men and six companions from Joppa to begin the 30-mile trip north to Caesarea. They arrive the following day.

- **Day 4, Caesarea**
Cornelius is eagerly anticipating the visit and has filled the house with friends and family. When Peter arrives, Cornelius falls at his feet, but the apostle tells him to stand up, since he's just a man too. The apostle states, "You yourselves know that it is unlawful for a Jew to associate with or visit a Gentile; but God has shown me I should not call anyone profane or unclean ... Now may I ask why you sent for me." **(Acts 10:28-29)** Cornelius tells his story, and the apostle preaches the Gospel to them.

While Peter is still speaking, the Holy Spirit falls on all the Gentiles and they begin speaking in tongues and praising God. "Then Peter said, 'Can anyone withhold the water for baptizing these people who have received the Holy Spirit just as we have?' So he orders them to be baptized in the name of Jesus Christ."

Cornelius and the Gentiles are baptized, and a new chapter in Christian history begins.

▲ *Peter the Apostle in the House of Cornelius*, a hand-colored woodcut of a 19th-century illustration by an unknown artist

---

PETER'S VISION
At this point in Acts, Peter still practices all aspects of his Jewish faith. He observes the Sabbath and keeps kosher laws and customs including the prohibition against eating with or entering the homes of Gentiles.

But after the vision of the sheet, Peter's views change. He no longer sees Gentiles as profane and welcomes Cornelius and other Gentiles into the faith.

The ruins of a church in ancient Shivta, a town built in the first century by Nabateans in the Negev Desert of Israel

WHEN ARE THE 12 DISCIPLES CALLED APOSTLES?

In the Gospels, Jesus's 12 closest associates are usually referred to as *disciples*, which means followers or learners. In Acts they are referred to as *apostles*, which means messengers or missionaries, since Jesus has sent them to preach the Gospel.

ACTS 11, 12, 15
A Major Controversy Develops

CHRISTIANS DEBATE WHETHER TO BAPTIZE GENTILES.

The vision the Spirit gives Peter on the rooftop, the meeting Peter has with the centurion Cornelius, and Cornelius's subsequent baptism have profound implications for the new faith.

Before Cornelius, all the followers of Jesus had been Jews. In the vision on the rooftop in Joppa, the Spirit of God makes it clear to Peter that the Gospel is not for Jews only but for all people.

Peter doesn't seem aware that his eating with Gentiles and accepting them as followers of Jesus would soon cause a major uproar among the believers. He also seems unaware that this one event would crack open the door for this new religion to break out of the Jewish communities it was born into and expand into all corners of the Roman Empire, and eventually the world.

REPORTING IN

Before Peter returns to Jerusalem, word has already reached the Church that he has baptized non-Jews into the faith. When he makes his report about what happened in Antioch, some believers criticize him saying, "Why did you go to uncircumcised men and eat with them?" (**Acts 11:3**) Peter retells the story of his encounter with Cornelius, including how the Holy Spirit fell on him and his household. When the apostles hear this, they praise God saying, "Then God has given even to the Gentiles the repentance that leads to life." (**Acts 11:18**)

THE CHURCH IN ANTIOCH

Around this time, because of increased opposition to believers in Judea, some followers of Jesus move north to the coastal area of Phoenicia, out to the Island of Cyprus, and to cities like Antioch of Syria.

When they arrive in these places, they preach only to other Jews. However, the believers start to preach the Gospel to non-Jews. In Antioch, for example, believers arrive from Cyprus and Cyrene who preach the Gospel to the Greek community. Many Greeks become followers of Jesus.

BARNABAS SENT TO INVESTIGATE

When the Church in Jerusalem hears about more Gentiles becoming followers of Jesus in Antioch, they send Barnabas, one of their leaders, to Antioch to investigate.

When Barnabas arrives in Antioch and spends time with the new Gentile believers, he is soon convinced that these new converts are indeed true followers of Jesus.

Barnabas wants to stay in Antioch and work among the new Gentile believers. Before he settles in, however, he goes to Tarsus to retrieve Saul (a recent convert who would soon be renamed Paul) to assist him in Antioch. Barnabas, now with Saul, returns to Antioch where they live for a year working in the growing church and teaching the new converts.

SURVIVING A DEATH THREAT

Meanwhile, back in Jerusalem, King Herod, alarmed by the growing number of followers of Jesus, thinks he can crush the movement by having James, the brother of John, arrested and beheaded. Then Herod has Peter arrested and makes plans to kill him after Passover. Word spreads that Peter is in prison, so the believers pray fervently for him.

▲ *The Baptism of St. Cornelius the Centurion* by Michel Corneille the Elder (17th century)

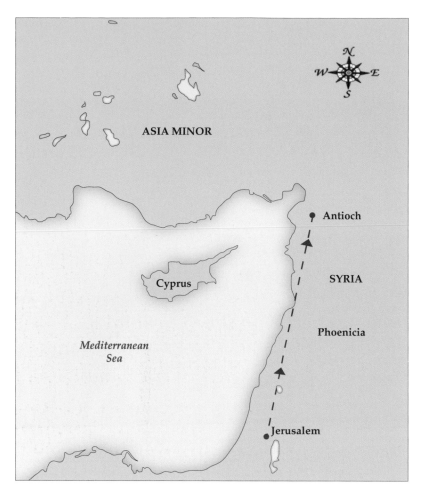

The Deliverance of St. Paul and St. Barnabas by Claude-Guy Hallé (ca. 1685)

▲ The debate about how Jewish should Gentile Christians be erupts in Antioch of Syria, shown in the map above.

WHO WAS JAMES?
He was the half-brother of Jesus and became a believer when he saw the resurrected Jesus. He rose to become the leader of the Church in Jerusalem and later wrote the book of James.

Peter, chained to two guards, is sound asleep when an angel appears in his cell, awakens him, and tells him to get up and get dressed. Peter follows the angel, thinking he's just dreaming. It is only once the iron gates open and Peter sees the angel suddenly leave that he knows he isn't having a vision and that he is actually free.

Peter goes to a believer's home where he knows Christians (followers of Jesus are first called Christians in Antioch of Syria) are praying for him. Peter knocks on the door. The maid, a young woman named Rhoda, recognizes his voice. She's so happy that Peter is free that she leaves him standing outside and runs to tell the others that Peter is at the door. They refuse to believe her. So Peter keeps knocking until they finally let him in. Peter then reports how God sent the angel

who released him from his chains and set him free.

THE INCIDENT AT ANTIOCH
Meanwhile, a serious issue arises in the church in Antioch. Some Jewish believers arrive from Judea and begin teaching that Gentile converts can't follow Jesus unless they are circumcised and follow the Law of Moses. The Greeks who had become Christians are especially appalled at this teaching as circumcision is repulsive in the Hellenistic culture.

Barnabas and Paul enter into a vigorous debate with these Judean proselytizers. But when they can't resolve the matter, they

all decide to go to Jerusalem and put the question before the apostles.

RESOLVING THE CONFLICT

The church leaders in Jerusalem welcome Paul and Barnabas and give them a chance to share all the ways God is blessing believers in Antioch. After they give their report, some former Pharisees who are now believers, protest saying, "Unless you are circumcised according to the custom of Moses, you cannot be saved." **(Acts 15:1)**

After a prolonged debate between the two sides, Peter stands up and reminds everyone of what happened when the first Gentiles became Christians. "God, who knows the human heart, testified to them by giving them the Holy Spirit just as he did to us; and in cleansing their hearts by faith he has made no distinction between us and them. . . . why are you putting God to the test by placing on the neck of the disciples a yoke that neither our ancestors nor we have been able to bear?" **(Acts 15:8-11)**

James announces the leaders' decision to accept Gentiles as they are and ask them only to refrain from any activities that would offend their Jewish brothers. While the controversy continues after this, the church leaders have made a decision that will help both sides get along with each other.

▲ *Saint James*, a detail of a Byzantine miniature from the *Code of Queen Constance*, Greek manuscript (12th century)

VERSE TO KNOW

"It is necessary for them [the Gentiles] to be circumcised and ordered to keep the law of Moses." (Acts 15:5)

CHAPTER 13

PAUL TRAVELS TO SPREAD THE WORD

Paul becomes a believer in Jesus. As a Roman citizen, he is free to travel throughout the Empire preaching about the new Christian religion.

Ruins of the Appain Way near Minturno, Italy. Paul most likely walked through here as he used the Roman road system extensively in his travels.

▲ When Saul is led into Damascus, he travels down Straight Street, shown here today.

WHAT IS A PHARISEE?
Saul was a Pharisee, a powerful Jewish sect that observed a strict interpretation of the law of Moses.

SAUL'S STORY

Born in Persia	ca. 5 B.C.
Educated and becomes a Pharisee	ca. 25–35 A.D.
At the stoning of Stephen	ca. 32–35 A.D.
Persecutes Christians	ca. 32–35 A.D.
Sees Jesus and is converted	ca. 35 A.D.

Standing among the crowd of rock throwers, a young Pharisee named Saul holds the coats of those stoning Stephen. Saul is a devout Jew living in Jerusalem who is known for defending Judaism at all cost.

In seeking to protect his faith, Saul searches out and persecutes Jews who follow Christ on grounds that they are blasphemers and should be punished.

A DRAMATIC CONVERSION
Saul embarks on a mission to halt the further spread of Christianity and asks a high priest for letters to the synagogues in Damascus. He plans to travel abroad, arrest believers in The Way, as Christianity is now called, and force them back to Jerusalem.

But as Saul nears Damascus, a bright light appears, shining around him, and he falls to the ground, blinded. "Saul, Saul, why do you persecute me?" a mysterious

voice asks. When Saul responds, insisting that the speaker identify himself, he hears these words: "I am Jesus, whom you are persecuting. But get up and go into the city, and you will be told what you must do."

Unable to see, Saul is led into Damascus,

where he spends three days neither eating nor drinking but only thinking about how wrong he has been about The Way and in persecuting Jesus's followers. He is then met by Ananias, a disciple of Jesus, who returns Saul's sight by the laying on of hands.

Saul is baptized and within a few days is proclaiming in synagogues that Jesus is the Messiah, the Son of God. From that day on, Saul preaches about Jesus with the same fervor he once used when he persecuted Christians.

▲ In *La Conversion De San Pablo*, an unknown artist depicts Paul falling from a horse. No such horse is mentioned in Acts 9.

St. Paul and St. Barnabas in Listri by Simone Peterzano (16th century)

PAUL'S FIRST JOURNEY

Barnabas and Saul begin first missionary journey	ca. 48 A.D.
John Mark abandons the trip and returns home	ca. 48 A.D.
The two men report to the church at Antioch	ca. 49 A.D.

ACTS 13, 14
The Roman Proconsul Converts

SAUL THE PERSECUTOR BECOMES PAUL THE MISSIONARY.

While Saul and Barnabas, another disciple, are serving Christians in Syria, the Holy Spirit tells church leaders in Antioch to send these men abroad to preach the Gospel. After fasting, praying, and laying hands on Saul and Barnabas, the leaders send the two out to spread the word throughout Galatia.

FIRST STOP: CYPRUS
Saul and Barnabas and a third traveler, John Mark, sail to the island of Cyprus, where Barnabas was raised, to begin their missionary

work. In Paphos, the three men meet with the Roman proconsul, Sergius Paulus, who wants to hear their message. A Jewish false prophet named Bar-Jesus interferes and tries to turn Paulus against his visitors.

Saul curses Bar-Jesus. "You son of the devil, . . . full of all deceit and villainy, will you not stop making crooked the straight paths of the Lord?" he says. "You will be blind for a while, unable to see the sun."

When Bar-Jesus then loses his sight, the proconsul is so astonished that he accepts the word of Jesus.

VERSE TO KNOW
"Set apart for me Barnabas and Saul for the work to which I have called them." (Acts 13:2)

The Ecstasy of St. Paul by
Nicolas Poussin (ca. 1643)

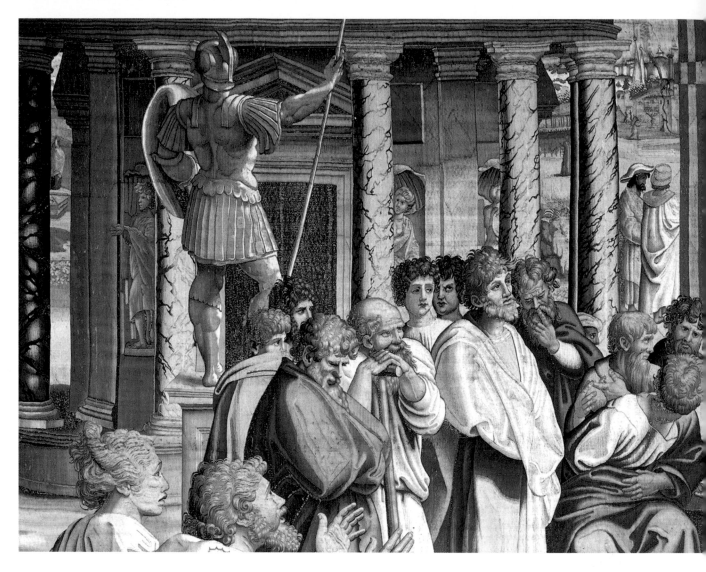

▲ *Saint Paul Preaching in Athens*, a panel from the series *Acts of the Apostles* (16th century)

ENERGIZING THE CROWDS

Paul and Barnabas sail to Perga on the Galatian mainland, where John Mark leaves them to return home, a departure which seems to anger Paul. With Barnabas, Paul proceeds to Antioch of Syria, where he speaks in a synagogue on the Sabbath and preaches the word of Jesus. His sermon is powerful and the following Sabbath, nearly the whole city comes to hear Paul's address. A group of Jews is offended by the challenge to their faith, and seek to discredit Paul and Barnabas.

When the missionaries are threatened with persecution, they leave, but some Jews and many Gentiles who remain in Antioch turn their faith to Jesus.

FIRST WORSHIPPED, THEN STONED

The pattern of preaching and persecution continues in Iconium and Derbe. When Paul encounters a man in Lystra who is lame from birth, he heals him. Excited by the miracle, the crowds want to worship Barnabas as the god Zeus and Paul as Hermes. The people prepare to sacrifice animals in honor of the "gods," but Paul vehemently protests that they are merely men, sent to bring good news.

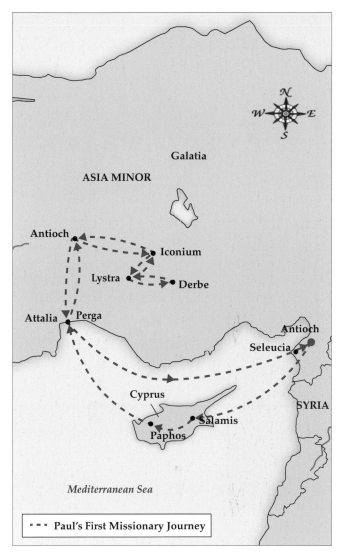

Paul's First Missionary Journey

▲ Paul most likely walked this colonnaded street in Perga, in what is now modern Turkey, during his missionary journeys.

The people, provoked by a group of visitors who arrive from Antioch and Iconium, turn on Paul and stone him until they think he's dead. But he revives and the next morning continues on to Derbe.

PAUL'S JOURNEY HOME

For three years Paul and Barnabas travel through the region preaching the Gospel, baptizing converts, and establishing churches.

When they finally return to Antioch of Syria, they tell the church leaders everything God has done with them.

▲ Paul leaves his home base in Antioch of Syria to evangelize and establish churches in Asia Minor— modern day Turkey.

▲ *St. Paul in the Areopagus,*
by Giovanni Ricco (1847)

———

VERSE TO KNOW
"These people who have
been turning the world
upside down have come
here also." (Acts 17:6)

ACTS 15–18
A Second Missionary Journey

PAUL MEETS TIMOTHY, WHO BECOMES A
FAITHFUL TRAVELING COMPANION.

———

Paul's next missionary journey gets off to a difficult start. He and Barnabas fight about bringing along John Mark, who created friction between Paul and Barnabas by abandoning the first trip. Barnabas decides to take John Mark and proceed to Cyprus to preach, while Paul takes Silas

and returns to churches from his previous journey.

TIMOTHY AND LUKE JOIN THE MISSION
In Lystra, Paul meets a young disciple named Timothy, whose mother is a Jewish believer and whose father is Greek. Timothy becomes Paul's faithful traveling companion and as close as a son.

Paul and Timothy attempt to preach the Word in synagogues and public arenas throughout Asia, but are forbidden twice by the Holy Spirit. While the men are in Troas on the Aegean coast, Paul has a vision during the night in which a man from Macedonia pleads with him for help. Paul, Luke, and Timothy realize the vision is a

▲ Albrecht Durer gathers four apostles together for his painting *Four Apostles*. *John Evangelist, Peter, Paul and Mark*. (ca. 1505)

significant one. God is directing them to the next place that they should preach about Jesus: Europe. They board a ship in Troas heading for Philippi, the closest port to Macedonia.

THE PHILIPPIAN JAILER

The group travels to Philippi. As Paul moves around the city preaching, he is followed by a fortune-telling slave girl who calls out, "These men are slaves of the Most High God, who proclaim to you a way of salvation." **(Acts 16:17)** Offended at the young girl's proclamation, Paul casts the evil spirits out of her.

After the encounter, the slave girl loses her fortune-telling powers and her owners are upset by the loss of income. In retaliation, they bring Paul and Silas before the local authorities and lodge false accusations. The missionaries are severely beaten and thrown into prison where a jailer leads them into the innermost cell and locks their feet in stocks.

About midnight, as Paul and Silas are praying and singing hymns, there is a violent earthquake; every prisoner's chains are unfastened and every cell door flies open. When the jailer sees the doors open, he assumes the prisoners have escaped and prepares to kill himself. But Paul stops the man, telling him the condemned are all still there. Trembling, the man asks Paul and Silas, "Sirs, what must I do to be saved?" **(Acts 16:30)** They tell him to believe in Jesus. Later, the jailer and all his family are baptized.

VERSE TO KNOW
"Believe on the Lord Jesus, and you will be saved, you and your household."
(Acts 16:31)

THE INCIDENT WITH THE SLAVE GIRL

Why does Paul get so upset at the fortune-telling slave girl? One theory is that she uses the indefinite article "a" instead of the definite article "the" when she says, ". . . who proclaim 'a' way of salvation." Paul rejects that there are multiple ways of salvation and so casts out the spirit within her.

▲ *Miracles of St. Paul at Ephesus* by an unknown artist (1693)

PAUL, ROMAN CITIZEN
Paul claims in Acts 22 that the treatment he has received is illegal because he is a Roman citizen, a Hellenistic Jew born in the province of Cilicia. At the time, Roman citizens had the right to appeal their case to Caesar in Rome.

VERSE TO KNOW
"Go, for I will send you far away to the Gentiles."
(Acts 22:21)

ACTS 19–28
Paul Spreads the Word

A MISSIONARY'S PRAYER IS ANSWERED
IN AN UNEXPECTED WAY.

Paul's deepest ambition has been to go to Rome and preach the Gospel in that great city. After returning from his third missionary journey, his dream finally comes true, though in a circuitous way.

PAUL'S THIRD MISSIONARY JOURNEY
Paul's next expedition takes him to Ephesus, where he preaches for two years. He is so successful that Luke proclaims that "all the residents of Asia, both Jews and Greeks, heard the word of the Lord." (Acts 19:10)

Eventually, however, rioters rise up against Paul and he leaves for Macedonia, Greece, and, over the objections of the prophets, for Jerusalem to celebrate Passover. The trip will prove a turning point for Paul.

ARRESTED IN JERUSALEM
One day while Paul is praying in the temple, Jews from Asia stir up the

crowd, which attempts to kill him. A Roman tribune rushes in with his soldiers to quell the commotion and takes Paul to the barracks.

Paul's nephew reports overhearing a jail plot to kill his uncle, and the Roman tribune uses 200 soldiers, 70 horsemen, and 200 spearmen to bring Paul to the governor of Caesarea.

Paul is held captive for two years, and when a new governor is seated, Paul's situation takes what seems to be a turn for the worse. He is accused by a lawyer for a high priest of being "a ringleader of the sect of the Nazarenes," **(Acts 24:5)** and of trying to profane the temple.

Paul defends himself, saying he has committed no offense. He asks to be sent to Caesar in Rome so his case can be heard. Along with other prisoners, Paul is entrusted to Julius, a centurion, and put on a ship for Rome where more adventures await.

▲ *Paul Before Felix* by William Hogarth (ca. 1752)

245

St. Paul of Tarsus Shipwrecked by Gustav Doré (19th century)

THE WRITING STUFF

Letters were composed on sheets of papyrus and attached end to end to make a parchment. The scroll for the book of Romans would have been about 13 feet long.

▲ New Testament writers including Paul wrote with split reeds or goose quills like the one shown here.

VERSE TO KNOW

"Do not be afraid, Paul; you must stand before the emperor. . ." (**Acts 27:24**)

PAUL'S LATER LIFE

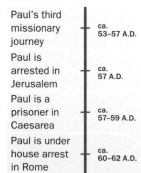

Paul's third missionary journey	ca. 53–57 A.D.
Paul is arrested in Jerusalem	ca. 57 A.D.
Paul is a prisoner in Caesarea	ca. 57–59 A.D.
Paul is under house arrest in Rome	ca. 60–62 A.D.

SURVIVING A SHIPWRECK

When the ship reaches the town of Fair Havens, Paul warns the centurion that the cargo, the boat, and the lives of all the passengers will be in danger if they continue. Julius chooses to proceed, and soon violent winds and waves pound the ship and the crew must throw both cargo and tackle overboard. The tempest rages for nearly two weeks and the soldiers and their prisoners begin to despair.

Paul hears from an angel that the travelers will be safe, and he encourages everyone to eat and be hopeful. The next morning, the ship is wrecked on rocks off the island of Malta and the soldiers want

to kill their captives. As Julius intervenes to save Paul, the passengers either swim or float on debris safely to shore and are greeted by locals, who build a welcoming fire. Trying to add wood to the blaze, Paul is bitten by a poisonous viper, but is unharmed. The event amazes the islanders, who hail Paul as a god. He, in turn, begins healing the sick.

A DREAM REALIZED

Once Paul arrives in Rome, he is allowed to stay in his own house and he welcomes everyone who visits. Paul has many opportunities to boldly preach about Jesus Christ, just as he has always dreamed.

Rembrandt's depiction of Paul writing in his prison cell in *Saint Paul in Prison* (ca. 1640)

ROMANS, 1 AND 2 CORINTHIANS, GALATIANS, EPHESIANS, PHILIPPIANS, COLOSSIANS, 1 AND 2 THESSALONIANS

Writing to Converts

PAUL'S LETTERS MAKE UP
MUCH OF THE NEW TESTAMENT.

Once Paul establishes a church and moves on, he doesn't forget about the new converts. To help them remain faithful to the Lord, he writes letters of encouragement and instruction from many different places and in various situations from approximately 50 A.D. through 67 A.D.

In total, 13 vibrant, brilliant letters are attributed to Paul. (A few may have been written by others working in his tradition.) They constitute nearly half of the New Testament.

GREAT WORKS

Here is a brief summary of epistles Paul composed to specific churches:

- **Romans,** written to the church of Rome, is considered Paul's greatest work, and is filled with doctrine. It focuses on salvation and how people are justified (made right with God) by faith, not works. It is also the only letter for a church that Paul didn't help start but hoped to visit someday.
- **1 and 2 Corinthians** are addressed to the church at Corinth, a cosmopolitan city known for its idolatry and vice. Because there are many problems in this mostly Gentile church, Paul seeks to correct the congregation's misdeeds and beliefs. Chapter 13 in the first letter contains his great teachings about love. The second letter is his most personal, as he declares his love for the people.
- **Galatians** is most likely composed during Paul's first missionary journey. It contains a powerful argument against the Jewish Christians, who insist that Gentile believers live by Jewish law.

In Galatians, Paul emphasizes grace and living by the power of the Holy Spirit.
- **Ephesians** (along with Philippians, Colossians, and Philemon) is written during Paul's first Roman imprisonment (60–61 A.D.). To the Christians at Ephesus, Paul declares the glorious mystery about "the church,

▲ In *St. Paul*, an unknown artist portrays Paul studying the Scriptures as he walks.

which is [Christ's] body," with Jesus Christ as the head of the church (1:22-23).

- **Philippians**, Paul's letter to the believers at Philippi, discusses happiness and unity in Jesus Christ. The letter itself is joyful, as Paul thanks his followers for helping him and reminds them of Christ's great sacrifice as he came to Earth to die for them.

- **Colossians** describes to believers in Colossae the person and work of Jesus as the creator, sustainer, and redeemer of mankind and the universe.

- **1 and 2 Thessalonians** are written about six months apart around 51 A.D. to the church in Thessalonica that Paul helps start in only three weeks time.

The first letter includes encouragement to stand fast and teachings about the second coming of Jesus. Paul writes 2 Thessalonians to comfort them as their persecution increases.

Saints Peter and Paul by Giovanni Baglioni (ca. 1600)

1 AND 2 TIMOTHY, TITUS, PHILEMON

Words of Wisdom

PAUL'S LETTERS CONTAIN THE BASIS FOR SOME OF CHRISTIANITY'S THEOLOGY.

Paul's letters, rich with advice, are written for two kinds of readers: church leaders seeking to build their congregations and individuals who want learn how to live as Christians. He also provides advice and guidance to the faithful.

ADVICE TO CHURCH LEADERS

These letters consider issues including how to treat a runaway slave.

- **1 and 2 Timothy** are addressed to Timothy, Paul's coworker and acolyte. The first letter is written to instruct him on how to lead and organize the local church in Ephesus effectively. The second letter is more somber in tone, as Paul has been imprisoned again and is facing execution. He hopes Timothy can come see him in Rome before Paul is beheaded, an event which eventually occurs in 67 A.D.

ADVICE TO INDIVIDUALS

Advice from Paul's missives on how to live, love, and treat others.

- **Titus,** written to his coworker about the same time as the first letter to Timothy, instructs Titus on how to correct issues developing in the Crete churches, as well as to warn him against false teachers.
- **Philemon** is the owner of a runaway slave named Onesimus, who has ended up in Rome and been converted by Paul. Now Paul sends him home to his master and encourages Philemon to receive his slave back with Christian kindness.

TIMELESS WORDS OF WISDOM

Advice in Paul's letters on various topics.

- **Confidence in Jesus:** "I can do all things through him who strengthens me." **(Philippians 4:13)**

In *Paul in Prison in Rome*, the unknown artist portrays Paul working with his assistant to pen his letter to the church in Ephesus. (1800)

- **Eternal Life:** "For the wages of sin is death, but the free gift of God is eternal life in Christ Jesus our Lord." **(Romans 6:23)**
- **Evil:** "Bless those who persecute you; bless and do not curse them. . . Do not be overcome by evil, but overcome evil with good." **(Romans 12:14, 21)**
- **Faith:** ". . . since we are justified by faith, we have peace with God through our Lord Jesus Christ." **(Romans 5:1)**
- **The Deity of Christ:** "In him the whole fullness of deity dwells bodily, and you have come to fullness in him, who is the head of every ruler and authority." **(Colossians 2:9-10)**
- **Love:** Love is patient; love is kind. . . [It] bears all things, believes all things, hopes all things, endures all things. Love never ends." **(1 Corinthians 13:4, 7-8)**
- **Peace Through Prayer:** "Do not worry about anything, but in everything by prayer and supplication with thanksgiving let your requests be made known to God. And the peace of God, which surpasses all understanding, will guard your hearts and your minds in Christ Jesus." **(Philippians 4:6-7)**
- **Second Coming:** "The Lord himself, with a cry of command, with the archangel's call and with the sound of God's trumpet, will descend from heaven, and the dead in Christ will rise first. Then we who are alive, who are left, will be caught up in the clouds together with them to meet the Lord in the air. . . ." **(1 Thessalonians 4:16-17)**
- **Unity:** "There is no longer Jew or Greek, there is no longer slave or free, there is no longer male and female; for all of you are one in Christ Jesus." **(Galatians 3:28)**

CHAPTER 14

THE GENERAL EPISTLES AND REVELATION

The last books of the Bible are organized in two sections. The first is eight letters, known as the General Epistles. The second section is Revelation, also called the Apocalypse, which is the New Testament's only instance of prophetic literature.

A 7th-century tapestry that depicts an angel giving John the Book of Revelation.

▲ *St. Augustine Reading the Epistles of St. Paul*, fresco at the Church of Sant Agostino, San Gimignano, Italy (1465)

AUTHOR, AUTHOR

For centuries, Church tradition held that Paul wrote Hebrews because the book was so heavily doctrinal. But some scholars now doubt that theory, in part because Hebrews suggests its author was an apostle, yet does not credit Paul. Speculation about other writers has ranged from Luke (possibly recording a sermon by Paul), Barnabas, Apollos, and Priscilla.

HEBREWS; JAMES; 1, 2 PETER; 1, 2, 3 JOHN; JUDE

The General Epistles

THE WRITINGS OF PETER, JOHN, JAMES, AND JUDE

Unlike most of the New Testament, which was written by Paul and which addresses specific people or churches, the "General Epistles," in the form of letters, were penned by other early Christians, and only 2 and 3 John are directed to specific individuals.

Each letter in the "General Epistles" is named after its most likely writer. James and Jude contributed one letter apiece.

The apostles Peter and John composed two and three letters respectively. The author of Hebrews is unknown. Here is a description of the content of each epistle.

- **Hebrews:** Because Jewish followers of Jesus are being persecuted, some are tempted to return to Judaism. This author emphasizes all the ways that the Christian covenant is superior to the Jewish one.
- **James:** Jesus's half brother has no use for hypocrites. He encourages Christians

to make their actions match their words and beliefs, writing, "faith without works is dead." (2:14-26)

- **1 Peter:** Aware of how Christians are suffering, Peter encourages them to be strong and to stay true to their faith.
- **2 Peter:** In this letter, Peter warns against false teachers, giving in to pride, and self-indulgence. Believing he will be martyred soon, Peter encourages readers to stay true to Jesus.

- **1 John:** Here, John also alerts believers against false teachers, as well as showing love for God by loving others.
- **2 John:** The letter addresses a woman and her children, encouraging them to walk in truth and not be misled.
- **3 John:** This brief letter is filled with gratitude to Gaius and others who were kind to John.
- **Jude:** This letter warns about falling away from the faith and reminds readers that rebellion brings punishment.

▲ *John the Evangelist and Mark Discussing Their Writings*, by an unknown artist

---

VERSE TO KNOW
"I write these things to you who believe in the name of the Son of God, so that you may know that you have eternal life." (1 John 5:13)

▲ *Christ in the Book of Revelation*, a miniature from the *Bible of Souvigny*, Latin manuscript (12th century)

REVELATION
The Final Word

THE LAST BOOK IN THE NEW TESTAMENT IS AN APOCALYPTIC VISION OF THE WORLD'S END.

Revelation, the last book of the New Testament and the entire Bible, is a prime example of apocalyptic literature.

Revelation is full of unfamiliar symbolism and horrific images of coming judgment on a sinful world. It also offers a panoramic view of God's plans and ends happily with John's vision of God's final victory over Satan.

Written in the last quarter of the first century, Revelation was meant to be a beacon of hope to Christians struggling against fierce persecution from Rome. The underlying message of Revelation is that no matter how bad things get, God is still in control, and evil will be defeated.

VISION OF JESUS CHRIST
John's vision begins with the appearance of the resurrected Jesus, who looks nothing like he did while on Earth.

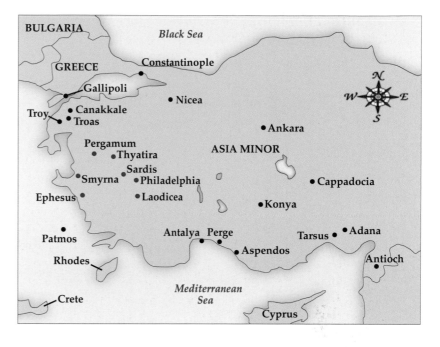

St. John the Evangelist at Patmos, from the *Mystic Marriage of St. Catherine Triptych* (1479)

▲ The seven churches of Revelation marked in red

His hair is white, his eyes blaze like fire, and he holds a double-edged sword in his mouth. The vision knocks John to the ground as if he has died. He is revived by Jesus's touch and told to write down the following messages for the churches.

SEVEN MESSAGES FOR SEVEN CHURCHES

Jesus uses John to rebuke the seven churches of Asia (see map).

- **Ephesus:** Jesus praises members of this church for how they deal with sinners, expose false teachers, and endure suffering. But he regrets they have abandoned the intensity of their first love for him.
- **Smyrna:** This church is as rich in faith as it is poor in worldly good. Jesus promises rewards to those who remain faithful, even during times of persecution.
- **Pergamum:** Reminding church members that he holds a two-edged sword, Jesus encourages his followers to repent of any sexual immorality and to take a stand against those who teach otherwise.
- **Thyatira:** Jesus names only one thing he has against this church: Its toleration of "that woman Jezebel," who claims to be a prophet but is leading the people into sexual sin.
- **Sardis:** "I know your works; you have a name of being alive, but you are dead." (Rev. 3:1) If they repent, members' names will remain in the Book of Life.
- **Philadelphia:** Praising this church for following his word and staying true to his name, Jesus promises to protect members in their hour of trial.
- **Laodicea:** Jesus accuses Laodicea of complacency and says he wants to spit members out of his mouth. Yet he stands at their door knocking, offering a chance.

OUT WITH A BANG
Apocalyptic literature typically presents a vision that reveals the end times. This style of writing is highly symbolic.

VERSE TO KNOW
"Do not fear what you are about to suffer. . . . Be faithful until death, and I will give you the crown of life." (Revelation 2:10)

REVELATION 4–8

A Scroll with Seven Seals

JOHN'S VISION MOVES FROM EARTH TO HEAVEN.

▲ *God the Father Enthroned* from the *Polyptych of the Apocalypse*, Galleria dell' Accademia, Venice, Italy (1343)

VERSE TO KNOW
"You are worthy to take the scroll and to open its seals, for you were slaughtered and by your blood you ransomed for God saints from every tribe and language and people and nation."
(Revelation 5:9)

WHY ARE THERE SO MANY SEVENS IN REVELATION?
In Hebrew symbolism, the number seven represents completion. So it's not unusual that the book that tells the story of God bringing human history to its completion would be filled with sevens. A partial list of the sevens in Revelation include churches, spirits, lampstands, stars, seals, horns, eyes, angels, trumpets, plagues, and golden bowls.

The action in Revelation chapters 4–5 moves from Earth to Heaven. John sees the door to Heaven standing open, and he hears the angel telling him to go in.

John sees God seated on a throne, engulfed in the beauty of rare gems and an emerald rainbow. Rumbles of thunder and flashes of lightning radiate from the throne as living creatures around God sing his praises and elders fall down before the throne to honor the Lord.

As John spots a scroll with seven seals in God's right hand, an angel asks, "Who is worthy to open the scroll and break its seals?" When no one can be found in Heaven and Earth, John weeps. Then Jesus Christ who John identifies as "a Lamb standing as if it had been slaughtered," comes forward and takes the scroll.

FOUR SEALS; FOUR HORSEMEN
The scroll Jesus holds will reveal God's plan for the unfolding of the end times. As each seal is broken, a series of judgments on the world cursed by sin is unleashed. The first four seals each reveal a horseman representing a specific type of punishment.

- **The White Horse.** This rider holds a bow and is given a crown. One interpretation is that he represents the beginning of the reign of the Antichrist, who obtains worldwide power and establishes a brief time of peace.
- **The Bright Red Horse.** Given a great sword, this rider initiates a time of war and great violence.

- **The Black Horse.** This rider, holding scales to measure food, seems to represent famine.
- **The Pale Green Horse.** The name of this rider is Death. He is given authority to kill one-fourth of the Earth's population with sword, famine, pestilence, and wild animals. He is followed by Hades, the abode of the dead.

SEALS FIVE THROUGH SEVEN

The fifth seal reveals the souls of Christians slaughtered for their testimony about Jesus. Their voices cry out for God to avenge their blood; they are told to have patience, and that vengeance will be accomplished.

With the sixth seal, God acts directly on the world. Following a great earthquake, the sun turns black, the moon looks like blood, and the stars fall to Earth. People are so terrified they hide in caves and ask to be hidden from the wrath of God.

Before the Lamb opens the seventh seal, there is silence in Heaven for half an hour. This dramatic pause builds the tension before God's wrath is unleashed in several more cycles of sevens with increasing degrees of punishment.

▲ *The Four Horsemen of the Apocalypse*, detail of the 16th century tapestry by Wilhelm Pannemaker

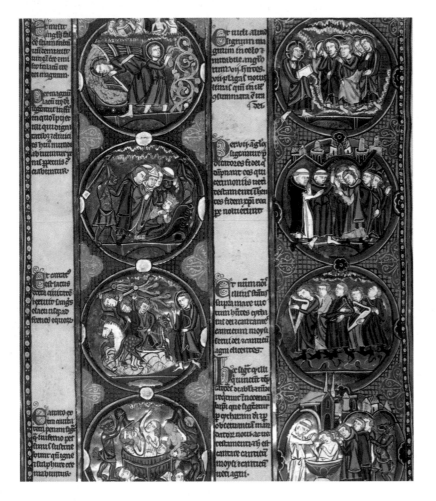

▲ Scenes from the Apocalypse, from *Bible Moralisee*, France (late 13th century)

———

VERSE TO KNOW
"Then I looked, and I heard an eagle crying with a loud voice as it flew in mid-heaven, "Woe, woe, woe to the inhabitants of the earth." (Revelation 8:13)

———

WHAT IS AN ANTICHRIST?
John is the only New Testament writer who uses the term *Antichrist*. It refers to one who stands in opposition to all that Jesus represents.

REVELATION 8–19

Divine Judgment

JOHN SEES TWO WITNESSES AND THREE MONSTERS.

———

John's vision includes a time of great tribulation culminating in a final battle, Satan's defeat, and Christ's triumphant return.

SEVEN TRUMPETS AND SEVEN BOWLS
Seven angels appear with seven trumpets. As each trumpet is blown, a new curse unfolds: hail and fire mixed with blood fall to Earth; a flaming mountain thrown into the sea destroys a third of the living creatures; the star Wormwood falls and turns the waters bitter; locusts that sting like scorpions descend from the skies; and plagues kill a third of humanity.

The seven bowls are worse than the seven trumpets. Painful sores pour from the bowls, water turns to blood, people are scorched by the sun's fire, darkness envelops the world, and a tremendous quake shakes the Earth. Even so, many people refuse to repent.

TWO WITNESSES
Before the seventh trumpet, God sends two witnesses to preach a message of judgment and repentance. Like Moses and Elijah, the witnesses have the powers to turn water to blood and call fire from Heaven. After three and a half years, a beast emerges from a bottomless pit and kills the witnesses. Their bodies lay on the streets for three and a half days before God resurrects them and takes them to Heaven. An earthquake kills 7,000 people, and those who remain give glory to God.

THREE MONSTERS
- **The Red Dragon** appears in a heavenly vision trying to devour an infant at the moment of birth. God saves both mother and child when the Archangel Michael and his flock attack the dragon, throwing him down to Earth. Enraged, Satan does everything he can to destroy the mother and her child.
- **The First Beast,** or the Antichrist, appears sporting 10 horns and seven heads. He blasphemes God and makes war on all his followers, setting up an earthly kingdom.
- **The Second Beast,** or the False Prophet, establishes a worldwide religion based on worship of the Antichrist. Anyone who refuses to worship him is killed. The two beasts make it impossible for anyone to buy or sell anything that does not have the name of the beast or his number (666) on his or her right hand or forehead.

DOCTORVM SAPIENS·ORDO

Sermon and Deeds of the Antichrist by Luca Signorelli from the Last Judgment fresco cycle (1499–1504)

▲ *The Whore of Babylon*, by Nicolas Bataille, from the Apocalypse of Angers, a medieval tapestry (ca. 1380)

REVELATION 17–20
Evil Is Destroyed

DRAGONS, A BEAST, AND BATTLES
AT THE END OF WORLD

No part of Revelation is more hotly debated than the sequence of events related to Christ's return, the final battle, and the 1,000-year reign of Jesus and his followers on Earth. Below is a summary of these events as they are recorded in Revelation.

THE FALL OF BABYLON

In the opening description, a prostitute on a scarlet beast rides in, representing the Antichrist's kingdom, known as Babylon. She holds in her hand a golden cup full of her abominations, and she is drunk with the blood of Christ's followers.

The prostitute is followed by ten Babylonian kings who join together to make war on the Lamb.

When the city of Babylon is destroyed by fire, the kings mourn, saying "Alas, alas. . . Babylon, the mighty city! For in one hour your judgment has come." **(Rev. 18:10)**

The Angel Binding Satan by an unknown artist (ca. 1797)

VERSE TO KNOW
"I also saw the souls of those who had been beheaded for their testimony to Jesus and for the word of God. They had not worshiped the beast or its image and had not received its mark on their foreheads or their hands. They came to life and reigned with Christ a thousand years." (Revelation 20:4)

THE BEAST IS DEFEATED

In the next passage, a rider on a white horse, whose name is "The Word of God," appears, followed by the armies of heaven.

The armies of heaven are attacked by the beast and the kings of the Earth, but it is the beast and the false prophet who fall. They are captured and are thrown alive into the lake of fire.

The rest of the beast's followers are killed by the rider's sword.

> "Satan is chained in a bottomless pit for a thousand years."

SATAN'S DOOM

Meanwhile, an angel seizes Satan and chains him in a bottomless pit for a thousand years. Those who have been martyred for their faith are resurrected and sit on thrones to reign alongside Christ on Earth until Satan's release. Once freed, Satan gathers an army to march on Jerusalem. But as the evil forces surround the city, fire comes from Heaven and destroys them. Satan is thrown into the lake of fire to be tormented day and night forever.

ENDING IT
This final conflict in the Bible is known as the Battle of Armageddon. Tradition says it will take place in the plain of Megiddo (below) in Israel.

Last Judgment by Jean Cousin the Younger (1585)

REVELATION 20-22

Eternity Begins

LIFE WITHOUT SIN AND THE DEVIL

Finally, evil has been defeated and Christ and the Church are triumphant. All that remains is the resurrection of the dead, the final judgment, and the creation of a new heaven and a new Earth where the redeemed will be forever with the Lord.

THE FINAL JUDGMENT

Revelation now moves to the spiritual realm, with God appearing on a great white throne. The dead are resurrected so God can judge their lives. Only those whose names are written in the Book of Life are admitted into Heaven. Other books are also opened, presumably to decide the degree of reward or punishment in the next life.

Since Death and Hades are no longer needed, they are cast into the lake of fire.

THE NEW JERUSALEM

With the old earth and heavens gone, John now sees a new Earth and Heaven appear. The New Jerusalem, the capital city of Heaven, comes down to become a dwelling place for the redeemed. God will live here among his flock and wipe tears from their eyes.

There is no longer any need for a sun or moon, since "the glory of God is its light, and its lamp is the Lamb." **(Rev. 21:23)**

This New Jerusalem, built entirely of crystal clear gold, has a high wall with 12 gates, inscribed with the names of the 12 tribes of Israel. The wall of the city has 12 foundations, with the names of the 12 apostles written on them.

THE RIVER AND THE TREE OF LIFE

The tree of life that was in the Garden of Eden reappears, and everyone has access to it. Each month the tree produces 12 kinds of fruit, and even its leaves bring healing.

Flowing from the throne of God down the main street of the city is the river of life, bright as the sun.

A PROMISE

In the final words of Revelation, John hears Jesus speak to him, "See, I am coming soon; my reward is with me, to repay according to everyone's work. I am the Alpha and the Omega, the first and the last, the beginning and the end." **(Rev. 22:12-13)**

Having seen all the glories of Heaven that will begin at Jesus's return, John says simply, "Amen. Come, Lord Jesus!"

▲ *The New Jerusalem*, a panel from a tapestry entitled *The Apocalypse of Angers* (1373)

VERSE TO KNOW

"And the one who was seated on the throne said, 'See, I am making all things new . . . To the thirsty I will give water as a gift from the spring of the water of life.'" (Revelation 21:5-6)

APPENDIX

OLD TESTAMENT

Pentateuch
1 Genesis
2 Exodus
3 Leviticus
4 Numbers
5 Deuteronomy

Historical Books
6 Joshua
7 Judges
8 Ruth
9 1 Samuel
10 2 Samuel
11 1 Kings
12 2 Kings
13 1 Chronicles
14 2 Chronicles
15 Ezra
16 Nehemiah
17 Esther

Wisdom Books
18 Job
19 Psalms
20 Proverbs
21 Ecclesiastes
22 Song of Solomon

Major Prophets
23 Isaiah
24 Jeremiah
25 Lamentations
26 Ezekiel
27 Daniel

Twelve Minor Prophets
28 Hosea
29 Joel
30 Amos
31 Obadiah
32 Jonah
33 Micah
34 Nahum
35 Habakkuk
36 Zephaniah
37 Haggai
38 Zechariah
39 Malachi

NEW TESTAMENT

Canonical Gospels
40 Matthew
41 Mark
42 Luke
43 John

Apostolic History
44 Acts

Pauline Epistles
45 Romans
46 1 Corinthians
47 2 Corinthians
48 Galatians
49 Ephesians
50 Philippians
51 Colossians
52 1 Thessalonians
53 2 Thessalonians
54 1 Timothy
55 2 Timothy
56 Titus
57 Philemon

General Epistles
58 Hebrews
59 James
60 1 Peter
61 2 Peter
62 1 John
63 2 John
64 3 John
65 Jude

Apocalypse
66 Revelation

INDEX

PHOTO CREDITS